PLANS, SPECIAL PROVISIONS AND CONTRACT PLAN REVIEWS

A Guide to Preparing a Set of Contract Plans and Special Provisions for an Infrastructure Project, and a Guide for Performing Contract Plan Reviews

PLANS, SPECIAL PROVISIONS AND CONTRACT PLAN REVIEWS

A Guide to Preparing a Set of Contract Plans and Special Provisions for an Infrastructure Project, and a Guide for Performing Contract Plan Reviews

BY

JACK SCHMITT, P.E.

A Red Pencil, Limited Production

Jack is a member of the Society of American Value Engineers. He has served as a text-book and pdh-course reviewer, a provider of exam problems to NCEES, is the author of a children's book as well as over a half-dozen on-line courses available through various pdh-providers.

Plans, Special Provisions and Contract Plan Reviews
A Guide for Plan Preparations, Writing Special Provisions
and Performing Plan Reviews

Copyright © 2006 by Jack Schmitt, P.E.

All rights reserved. No part of this book may be reproduced or transmitted in any form or by any means, electronic or mechanical, including photocopying, recording, or by any information storage and retrieval system, without permission in writing from the copyright owner.

Library of Congress Control Number: 2007923613

ISBN: 978-1-59824-440-3

First Edition
Published February 2007
E-BookTime, LLC
6598 Pumpkin Road
Montgomery, AL 36108
www.e-booktime.com

Contents

Foreword 9

Chapter One PREPARING INFRASTRUCTURE PLANS............ 17
   The Cover or Title Sheet 17
      The Project Title 18
      Jurisdiction and Funding Sources 20
      Project Identification Numbers 21
      Project Maps 23
      Design Data 27
      Route Designation or Classification 29
      Pavement Type 29
      Design Speed and Posted Speed 30
      Responsible Parties 31
      Agency Approval 31
      Funding Source Approval 32
      Licensed Professional Seal 32
      Miscellaneous Information 33
   The Index Sheet 39
   The General Notes Sheet 42
   The Summary of Quantities Sheet 45
   The Schedules of Quantities Sheet 50
   The Typical Sections Sheet 54
   The Construction Layout Sheet 61
      Alignment 61
      Ties 62
      Benchmarks 66
   The Traffic Control Sheet 69
      Construction Sequencing or Staging 69
      Detour Plans 76
      Construction Access 76
   The Plan Sheet 79

Contents

The Profile Sheet 83
The Drainage Sheet 85
The Utility Relocation Sheet 89
The Grading Sheet 90
The Cross-Section Sheet 93
The Construction Detail Sheet 96
Miscellaneous Sheets 98
The Sediment Control / Erosion Control Sheet 100
    Sediment Control 100
    Erosion Control 101
The Landscaping Sheet 103
The Signing and Pavement Marking Sheet 106
Right of Way Plans 109

Chapter Two WRITING SPECIAL PROVISIONS 111
    Introduction 111
    Format 112
    Types of Special Provisions 113
        General 113
        Construction 114
        Performance 115
        Regulatory 115
    The Grammar of a Special Provision 116
        Description 117
        Location 118
        Means 118
        Materials 119
        Measurement 120
        Basis of Payment 121

Contents

Chapter Three PERFORMING CONTRACT PLAN REVIEWS .. 124
   Introduction 124
      Field Check 126
      Team Meetings 127
      Sheet Reviews 128
      Anomalies 128
      Questions for Reviewers 129
      Title Sheet 131
      Index of Sheets 132
      General Notes 133
      Summary of Quantities 134
      Schedules of Quantities 135
      Typical Sections 136
      Layout and Alignment 137
      Benchmarks 138
      Traffic Control 138
      Paving Plans 140
      Profiles 141
      Drainage 142
      Grading 144
      Utilities 145
      Cross-Sections 145
      Construction Details 147
      Traffic Signals 147
      Lighting 148
      Erosion Control 149
      Landscaping 149
      Signing 150
      Pavement Marking 150
      Right-of-Way Plans 150
About the Author 151

Foreword

Engineers, architects and contractors communicate with each other, with their clients, and with the construction trades by using words, numbers, lines and symbols which follow a format that is unique to a region, an agency or a funding source. The content and layout of each sheet or drawing in a set of contract plans has evolved over the years to adapt to the various end uses of the documents, as well as the manner in which storage and retrieval of the documents occurs. Over the past twenty years, the methods of drawing preparation have undergone radical transitions, progressing from the use of ink on starched linen, through the use of plasticized lead on film, then to the use of computer-aided design and drafting by electronic means, inkjet plotting and on to magnetic diskette or optically-programmed disks. Through all of these cycles of transition, the purpose of the drawings as a communication tool has remained unchanged. The intent of the drawings was and will continue to be, the conveyance of design intentions and directions of a specialized nature to a skilled tradesman or builder. The recipient construction contractor in the field may have performed similar work for many years, or may be a novice who is attempting an initial venture into the construction industry. In any situation, the need for concise, precise communication remains unchanged.

As the staff at jurisdictional agencies has matured and moved upward through the ranks, as design firms and construction firms have undergone staff rotation, promotions and acquisitions, as funding sources

Foreword

and programs were initiated and completed, one underlying element of the process went un-noticed. The formal training of engineers in the preparation of construction drawings became less a function of the institutions of higher education, and more a function of on-the-job experience under the tutelage of an experienced individual. At the same time, the numbers of students entering the field of infrastructure and transportation-oriented civil engineering has not kept pace with the numbers of practicing engineers who have moved to the managerial side of the practice or retired completely from active service. Consequently, the responsibility for on-the-job training has fallen to fewer and fewer individuals in each firm, while the workload has reflected the need for more narrowly-focused, specialized input into each set of plans. The result often leads to a scramble for the last similar set of plans prepared by departed staff members for reference as a sample. In other instances, a request is made of the client to provide a sample set of plans prepared by another firm for a similar situation.

It is a recognized cost of doing business to expend time, effort and budget to pursue an assignment, to meet with the client for interviews or discussions about a potential project, to prepare an estimate and a proposal describing an approach to a project, to negotiate a fee and finally to execute an agreement for professional services. Then there is the time and effort to enter the new project into the various accounting systems to track the labor and internal costs, monitoring systems to manage the assigned staff and reporting systems to generate an invoice. In most instances, not one second of time in all of these activities results in a single usable drawing that can be inserted into the final set of plans. Nor is there a line item included to educate the staff in the preparation of a set of plans consistent with the expectations of the client, since the client selected the firm based on their qualifications, their reputation in a particular service or their previous performance.

Foreword

The negotiated fee might include an amount of time to assemble the project team and define the task, the schedule and the importance of generating a product worthy of the reputation of the firm. The fee will most likely reflect an amount of time to perform a specific task based on an estimate of effort required, based on a comparison to a similar recent assignment of equal magnitude. The fee may also include a number of hours for internal checking by each of the disciplines involved, such as the drainage, roadway, electrical, mechanical, construction and structural sections. An estimate is sometimes included to allow for revisions requested by the client. However, in most cases, the fee does not include a number of hours to re-design an element of the project necessitated by a loss of internal communication between disciplines. Situations such as ditches passing through bridge piers, sewer lines passing through temporary retaining walls, traffic signal controllers placed in roadside ditches, light poles placed on top of manholes, construction staging that contradicts standard practice for underground operations, and sign foundations in driveways or through shallow culverts are examples of the unintended conflicts that are sometimes shown using an overlay of the various plan sheets, and all too often are not addressed until the contractor is ready to perform the proposed activity. These and many other similar situations have simple preventions. The drawings and project documents may be reviewed by another experienced staff member in the firm, who may have performed some of the design, but was not involved in the preparation of the drawings. This somewhat disassociated person can often spot anomalies that will need attention to avoid change orders or unpleasant meetings with a disappointed client.

Some firms maintain a library of sample plans, policies and procedures to follow during the course of the preparation of plans. Some firms compile an internal manual that describes the use of computer-aided systems, software programs and manual checking procedures to use in

Foreword

order for a product to be readily acceptable to the client. Still other firms follow the same procedures time and again, until the original reasons for the format or content are lost but never challenged or altered. The responsibility to ensure that all members of the project team have access to the same information falls on some staff member between the top level of management and the project engineer/manager. An explanation of the format of the plan sheets is sometimes assumed to have occurred, but given the ongoing, prevalent need to perform revisions to the plan sheets to meet a client's requirements, a general overview of the nature, intent and content of each sheet does not occur simply by providing a project team with a sample set of plans from another project. Direction and mentoring is required from an experienced staff member to ensure success.

I have never encountered a set of plans in which I could not find a drawing that depicted a situation which contradicted the rest of the plan sheets. It usually takes less than an hour to find something that could be costly if not addressed. It is not just the grammar, the missing pay item or the garbled note or special provision. It is usually a contradiction that was not intended, but was not found using the traditional intra-discipline review. The existence of such anomalies is a reflection of the complex assembly of talent and design skills needed in order to complete a set of contract plans. The experienced person upon whose talent the firm was selected to provide engineering services may not have been in a position to provide the overall review before the plans were submitted. Such a situation may be readily apparent to the contractor preparing a bid, and the contractor may call in and question the issue. In some instances, time does not permit the preparation and distribution of an addendum. This usually leads to a construction change order and possible delays while action is taken by the community's governing body to approve the added expenditure. Twenty years ago, change orders totaling two to five percent were in

Foreword

the acceptable range. Today, we might be seeing totals in the twenty percent range. There is no need for that to happen. It cannot be reversed overnight, but a reversal can begin. It is my intent to share the knowledge base I have gathered in order to provide a beginning for that reversal. Project budgets and the insurance policies of the consulting industry cannot afford to do other than to take the steps toward that reversal.

The primary goal of this publication is to describe the logic and purpose of each of the Sheets or Drawings in order to assist the practicing engineer in the preparation of a cogent communication tool that is biddable, constructible and durable as a reference source. It is intended to serve the Project Manager or Project Engineer who has been assigned the task of producing a set of plans for a client's project, but who has had limited experience in performing such a task. This text will involve an examination of the content, layout and depth of information provided on each sheet or drawing. The examples represent a typical roadway project. The plan preparation process can be applied to a sewer project, a parking lot, a water-main project or any of a number of types of infrastructure improvements. Similarities between a set of roadway plans and a set of electrical, mechanical or site development plans will be evident to engineers in those disciplines.

The secondary goal is to provide the practicing engineer with examples of the various ways in which the normal course of events can lead to the unintentional expenditure of limited budget dollars, resulting in the need for last-minute revisions, or worse – the production of an end product that does not appear to be the seamless expression of excellence that the client was expecting to receive. It is more cost-effective to perform a specific task once, within the budgeted labor dollars, than to have to expend additional labor dollars to re-direct efforts or repeat tasks that have somehow reached a different concluding point than the

Foreword

rest of the project. It is certainly understood that it is better to catch the "glitch" and resolve the "anomaly" in-house before the end product reaches the client, since it is easier to maintain a reputation for excellence than it is to restore a reputation that is brought into question by a set of plans that contains contradictions, mismatches or unresolved cross-references that could lead to questions during construction. Furthermore, it would be much harder to request the inclusion of labor dollars for a "quality assurance program" in a future proposal for professional services if the previous assignment, using that same "quality assurance program", resulted in a product with questionable or unreliable contents.

The third goal is to provide a base from which staff can be trained to ask the proper questions, utilize the response in the appropriate manner, and realize the necessity to verify information with other disciplines as well as to advise other disciplines when designs, line-work, sequencing of operations or scope of work has been altered.

While this guide is not intended to serve as a template for the development of plan checking procedures, the text offers suggestions that may be helpful in the development of a quality assurance program that can be beneficial in reducing the expenditure of labor dollars to perform the correction of lines, numbers and symbols which were placed on the plan drawings with considerable forethought, but must be revised in order to conform to the expectations of the client.

Many clients use in-house resources to prepare a set of plans in response to a need that cannot be filled through a consultant selection process. The engineering staff of a client such as a public agency may find this text useful, as knowledge bases change through retirement, attrition, promotion, reduction-in-force, or any of a number of situa-

Foreword

tions that result in a loss of resources that could mentor someone in the preparation of plans.

It is left to the reader to ascertain the potential that this text represents within each firm, organization, or agency.

Chapter One

PREPARING INFRASTRUCTURE PLANS

The Cover or Title Sheet

Most projects use a Title or Cover Sheet for identification purposes. For some jurisdictions or clients, a set of contract documents may be abbreviated to the degree that an official Title Sheet or Cover Sheet is not used. It is entirely possible for most of the information that might be contained on a formal Title or Cover Sheet will be included somewhere in the plans or contract documents. For the remainder of this text, the term "Title" will mean the Title and the Cover Sheet, as well as the "Lead" Sheet, "Sheet One" or any number of individualized terms in use by various agencies to identify the first or initial identification page of a set of construction plans.

The Title Sheet contains various labels, identifiers and information that will be useful to the agency funding the project, the contractor constructing the project and future designers looking for reference data that may help on other projects. The Title Sheet usually indicates a number of unique aspects of the project, including: the official name of the project; identification of the type of work to be performed and the funding program or source of money that is being drawn upon; a map or sketch showing the relationship of the project to the regional and local street network; an indication of the length of, or the area of the project; the name of the responsible agencies or design professionals involved in the preparation and administration of the project, and, in some instances, the Title Sheet may serve as a display area for such elements as the Index of Sheets or Plan Content, General Notes, public and private utility contacts, scales of the various drawings, and the delineation of labor union and permitting jurisdictions.

The Project Title
The name of a project typically begins in the early planning stages, with the establishment of initial funding for studies or preliminary engineering. On rare occasions, as a project evolves, the nature of the final improvement may not exactly match the name of the project. For instance, a streetscape project may be determined to require pavement patching and then ultimately become a complete pavement reconstruction, but in order to monitor the status of the project by any of a number of interested individuals within the funding agency, the original name of the project could very well remain constant. For another example, a project may begin as a roadway-resurfacing endeavor with an add-lane condition at an intersection. By the time that preliminary studies are complete, the project may have grown into one that includes a bridge replacement, a segment of complete pavement reconstruction and traffic signal modifications. It may not always serve the best interests of the funding entity to change the name of the project as additional work becomes necessary. Therefore, it is typical for the project title to resemble the wording of the initial project title, perhaps using the term "resurfacing" in some fashion, but also include terms for bridge and traffic signal work, which might not be included in a project entitled "resurfacing". The additional work would undoubtedly exceed the initial estimates for the project, which in turn could result in a formal name change as additional funding sources are applied. In some jurisdictions, the original project title or number or description remains from start to finish of the entire engineering process from preliminary or conceptual design, to final contract document preparation.

Plans, Special Provisions and Contract Plan Reviews

Over time, based on funding constraints, the project might actually be divided into component parts. In such a case, each component would represent a particular specialty, such as roadway reconstruction, bridge replacement and traffic signal modifications. Each component could then become a separate set of plans, or the various components might become a sub-stage of the original resurfacing project, linked by completion dates to ensure a seamless progression of work.

Typically, a multi-disciplined project will involve various staff members representing individual specialties. The project could be renamed or categorized internally within the design firm, using a label understood by the firm's managing department. This process often results in the placement of a project name on an individual sheet within the plan set that is completely different from the project name that will appear on the Title Sheet. In many firms, it is common practice to label the product of a specific discipline, such as a drainage project, using a recognizable term. A client may have independent reasons for wanting to call the drawings by specific names. For instance, the engineers and technicians performing the design of the lighting segment may call it "electrical" work. The client may wish to refer to the sheets showing this work as "roadway electric plan" or "unit duct layout". If the internal staff applies their common term to the drawing rather than using the client's preferred term, the client might have the impression that the work has passed out of the control of the project manager. This is evident when the client offers a review comment asking to use their terminology in the work produced.

The in-house process that may help avoid the expenditure of labor dollars to revise the project title that is used on the Title Sheet, as well as the project title that is used on any other sheet within the set of plans, can be quite simple. The project title might be within the Request for Proposals or in the Request for Qualifications. The project title could be in the Advertisement for Services or in an invitation to bid for Design-Build Services. However, the project title used in the initial pre-engineering period might not be the same as that used in the actual Agreement for Engineering Services. Therefore the Agreement for Engineering Services could define the engineering to be performed in general terms, but would most likely contain the official project title. Often, the representatives of the firm involved in signing the agreements are not the same as the individuals involved in the preparation of the pre-engineering submittals. Sometimes, when the firm is about to begin work, the representatives of the firm who attend the initial project kick-off meeting with the client may not be the same as the actual team members who will produce the work. In any case, the client can identify the official project title at any of the project initiation meetings. The firm then needs to advise all participants of the official name of the project and direct the staff to use the project name on all correspondence, all invoices and all sheets within the set of plans.

Jurisdiction and Funding Sources

The Title Sheet will often indicate the hierarchy of authorities or jurisdictions having an interest in the project by virtue of their governmental capacity, ownership of the property upon which the project is constructed, or ultimate responsibility for the management and operation of the completed project. The project funding and approval may take place at a number of levels and be approved by various agencies or jurisdictions. It is common to display the names of these agencies at the top of the Title Sheet, in descending order or hierarchy or proportion of funding. This listing could include the federal government, state, county, borough, parish, commonwealth, district, township, city, town, village, political precinct or management association. The listing may also acknowledge the priority for approval, or serve as a means to help identify the project as a local, regional or multi-state endeavor. It is possible for a project to commence with funding at the local level, and then to receive infusions of funding at various other levels of government or taxing jurisdictions, until the end product may consist of a

Plans, Special Provisions and Contract Plan Reviews

Title Sheet that identifies a number of agencies whose funding has been utilized. "Ownership" or control of the project by the originating agency or client may remain unchanged.

The preferences of each client will differ regarding the ranking of the various governmental entities involved. The list might reflect the percentage of involvement, the relative liabilities incurred, or the political rankings in either ascending or descending order. An in-house process that may help to avoid exceeding the budget for the preparation of the Title Sheet would involve the preparation of a sample listing for discussion with, and concurrence from the client, thereby ensuring a minimum of revisions to the Title Sheet, since many clients allow only a few hours of effort for the preparation of this part of the work, but the end product may be revised several times as new information becomes available. A single confirmation meeting with the client would therefore save many hours of un-necessary revisions.

Project Identification Numbers

Many agencies and clients utilize a numbering system as the means of identification for a project. Numbers become reference tags for the various agencies to track budgets, progress and status. This identification number may change during the various phases or stages of a project, so it is common for a project to have a unique number when it originates, a separate number when it reaches conceptual approval, another number at plan preparation and a new identification number for construction. Some agencies use the same number from beginning to end in order to ensure that a project can refocus in a different direction without losing its identity within an accounting system. For some agency program staff, it is far easier and more cost-effective to re-define a project than to re-name or re-number it in a budget tracking system.

The numbering system may involve terms or labels such as job number, section number, project number, contract number, or other terms including fiscal year allocation, budget, line item, tracking system, appropriation, letting, or program. Each has a particular and unique origin, and each has a specific meaning to the agency. In most cases, the identification number is not interchangeable between terms and labels. The number may undergo subtle changes as the project advances from the preliminary to the final stage. A working knowledge of the derivation and meaning of the identification number is essential to ensure that it is in its proper place during design.

Given that the identification number is unique to the project, regardless of whether it refers to the project status, design job number, construction funding source or program year, the Title Sheet is the logical place for the display of all of the numbers, in the exact format that the agency prefers to see them listed, which have any bearing on the nature or development of the proposed improvement. This may include all manner of punctuation, hyphenation, brackets and spaces between letters and numbers. Often, the identification number appears in a specific manner or location on each of the drawings within the set of plans. The number may also be in bold font, italics or specific lettering size.

To avoid having to revise the project number on the Title Sheet as well as on the various other sheets or locations within the set of plans, the firm performing the work will need to understand the numbering system of the agency, the preferences of format for the number and the location for the number to be placed on a sheet. This also requires that the firm communicate the number to all disciplines involved in the project, as well as the firm's internal accounting and invoicing staffs. This will ensure that each transmittal to the client is identifiable for processing by the recipient departments. The need for this type of coordination becomes apparent on a multi-disciplined project, where each group of staff members involved in a unique specialty could generate drawings and reports using the identification number in a variety of forms and formats. Structural teams will often use an initial project

Plans, Special Provisions and Contract Plan Reviews

number for their preliminary submittal, and will retain the use of this number throughout the entire design process. This can result in last-minute revisions of each Sheet produced by a design discipline in order to comply with the client's system.

Project Maps

The Title Sheet will typically contain a map to locate the project. The type and scale of the map will vary based on the client. In some cases, more than one map may help identify the project within various jurisdictions. A quick glance will show a state official, such as a member of the elected representative body, state maintenance or policing agency, or a labor-related official, where the project is located in order to determine whether action, reaction or acknowledgement is required. A prospective bidder on the project can use the mapping to identify the relative proximity to staging areas, supply sources, borrow pits or dump sites. The prospective bidder can also determine the surrounding access conditions. A project map can be used to provide an indication of the relative length of the proposed improvement.

State or County Map

If a project is subject to federal or state funding, a statewide map will typically be included in order for the appropriate federal and state agency officials to quickly identify the work within their district or area of responsibility. Given the wide range of services provided at the state and federal levels, an agency may be involved or affected without having been in direct contact with the firm performing the design services or the client originating the assignment. This could include environmental agencies, interstate commerce commissions, regional planning coordinators and various bureaus whose databases will be affected or will require updating to reflect the project. There is interagency overview at various levels of government, but no singular entity can have all knowledge of all projects from the public and private sectors in any one region which might be taking place at any given time. It would be most undesirable to allow the implementation of an improvement to have a negative impact on the regional transportation network. So, for that reason, a simple mark on a state-shaped map provides a macro-view that can suffice as a prompt to allow the exchange of critical information regarding projects which may overlap in a specific area.

Local Project Map
The bidder or prospective contractor will focus on the micro-view of the project, typically presented as a location map or local sketch or roadway system map. This map identifies the project limits, the interaction with the local street network, the orientation of the project with regard to political boundaries such as city limits, county or township lines, and the survey terms such as USGS range and township so that other available mapping can be obtained in an efficient manner.

The interaction with the local street network would allow the potential contractor to see the access routes to the project, which might involve crossing railroad tracks, congested highways or bridges over waterways which may have seasonal delays. It would be beneficial for the location map to show all streets in the project area. However, each agency has its own requirements and it is common for a project location map that is used for a state or county project to have a different focus on the street network than the map used for a local municipality or township. All mapping would not be to the same degree of detail in every project, but it is typical to show all of the numbered routes, interchanges and intersecting streets as a minimum. The potential bidder will most likely visit the project site as a prelude to compiling an estimate of the costs involved in constructing each component part of the project. Access or delivery routes, areas for the field office, worker parking and material storage, overhead electric power and telephone lines, viaducts and heavy traffic generators would not necessarily be

Plans, Special Provisions and Contract Plan Reviews

shown on the location map, but would be observed by the potential bidder during a visit to the project site. The contractor and suppliers may be approaching the project from all directions, at various times of the day, and will need to be able to prepare a bid based on the realities of dealing with all physical parameters associated with the project site in order to be able to complete the project within the timeframe indicated in the proposed schedule.

The project might cross municipal, township or county lines, affecting labor rates, engaging various ordinances which might affect hours of operations, interrupt routine seasonal maintenance or impose noise restrictions. School District boundaries may also affect the hours of operations, since certain streets in the project area may contain bus-loading areas. Schools or Park Districts may have athletic fields within the immediate vicinity of a project, which would in turn affect the use of streets in the area. The location of a project will also necessitate an understanding of the jurisdictional boundaries for emergency services, public transit and school bus routes, in order to schedule the timely arrival of materials to the jobsite, such as asphalt and concrete. Delays in arrival affect the placement of such time and temperature-sensitive materials. Forest Preserve District boundaries may also cross the project, initiating ordinances or regulations that could affect native flora and fauna.

A roadway-based map is not the only document that identifies the properties of a project area. By providing the township and range on the project location map, the prospective bidder can easily reference aerial-based photographic mapping, as well as soil conservation district documents to assist in locating borrow pits, areas under construction and drainage features. A project might require borrow or disposal of excess excavation, which will require an assessment of the logistical needs for access and return routing. A project that is affected by a nearby waterway might be augmented by a map that delineated the anticipated high-water elevation of record so that sufficient planning could take place to avoid flood damages. An overview or knowledge of the direction from which overland flow will arrive, and an identification of the downstream recipient of project runoff will assist in determining the frequency of maintenance and replacement of erosion control systems, avoiding seasonal events which could adversely impact operations. A map showing the soils of the area will inform the prospective bidder of the nature of the underground material which might be encountered. Many categories of information and knowledge of the surrounding area are essential in the preparation of a competitive bid.

To be of sufficient practical use, at a minimum, the location mapping will need to identify the project limits against the background of the local street system. Regional roadway systems such as expressways and interchanges can assist in guiding the prospective bidder to the project site. The information conveyed by the location map or sketch will be enhanced with the inclusion of political or survey labels to help find other maps which might be of use to augment the preparation of a bid or to see the proximity of projects underway by other agencies. Providing the length of the improvement may help a potential bidder identify whether the project is of sufficient size to warrant the investment of resources to prepare a bid. Revisions to the map can be avoided through a discussion of the anticipated usage of the map with the client, by comparing the map to that shown on similar projects in the area, and by comparing the latest roadway mapping available with aerial photography and a field visit. Incorrect geographic placement of a project on a regional map can lead to revisions in construction staging, traffic detours and unintended labor hours in other parts of the plans. The project design team sometimes gets their jobsite knowledge from a photo log, and sometimes the project budget only allows one field trip to the jobsite. For projects of multiple-year duration, a person who made the visit or who took the photos could leave or be re-assigned. Jobsite knowledge can be lost during a project.

Plans, Special Provisions and Contract Plan Reviews

Design Data

The Title Sheet can convey basic design criteria for a roadway, which in turn serves as a guide or prompt for scheduling future maintenance operations. The criteria listed will not always reflect design criteria for internal elements such as drainage and landscaping. On the other hand, when the criteria identifies the intended design service life and the anticipated usage of the road, it can serve as a quick reference in the event that traffic were to be routed onto the project as part of a future detour that might be contemplated to allow expedient construction of another project. It is not infeasible for a detour to adversely impact a roadway that had not been intended to handle a high volume of traffic. The design criteria for a water-main, sewer or culvert can also be useful as a quick reference for assessing the type of materials that may be required for construction.

Design Year

Projects can be designed to serve the public for a specified number of years. A Drainage project involving a ditch may be expected to serve for a different length of time than a Drainage project involving a sewer pipe. A sanitary sewer project might be dependent on the anticipated daily loading that is to be temporarily conveyed during construction. A Bridge project may have components that are intended to endure for 50 years, while a mixed-use pedestrian / bike path could be expected to provide service for 25 years. The timeframes will depend on the local jurisdiction as well as industry guidelines.

Roadway projects are designed to serve traffic for a specific timeframe, known as the design life, which designates the intended service life of the pavement. This period of service, typically measured in units of axle loadings, but often stated in years, is based on the anticipated average annual traffic. In some jurisdictions, the design period serves to trigger implementation of routine inspection, pavement rating and programming of future budgets to ensure pavement maintenance. Even though a pavement may have a design life of 20, 30 or more years, the surface of the pavement may need routine maintenance in order to ensure that the intended friction factor is provided for the service life of the pavement. For an agency using a comprehensive pavement maintenance program, the Design Year data assists in the calculation of the estimated future costs of pavement rehabilitation.

Some pavements serve a limited number of heavy-axle and tandem-trailer vehicles over their service life. This number could be presented on the Title Sheet in one of several related terms, which could be the Average Daily Traffic (ADT), the Design Hourly Volume (DHV), the Traffic Factor (TF), Average Multiple Units (MU) anticipated in the design period or the Maximum Hourly Volume (MHV). There is a direct correlation between pavement design and the number of axle loadings anticipated to be received during the design life. In the event that the anticipated number of axle loadings occurs prior to the design life, the pavement will begin to fail, resulting in the need for attention by the maintaining agency prior to the date or time at which such work was anticipated or programmed. Premature pavement deterioration can also be the cause of vehicle incidents, which in turn can engage the designer in legal issues that were not anticipated.

The Design Year is a future date that is determined during the concept stage of a project. In some instances, based on policy modifications and the impacts of local development, the Design Year can change to a later future date during the plan preparation stage. Since the Design Year can affect the pavement typical section and in turn affect the content of various drawings within a set of plans, it is necessary for various design disciplines to routinely verify the Design Year in order to avoid spending labor budget to revise other drawings in the plans that depend on this information. This becomes more critical if a project involves a bridge, since the design loadings may vary depending on the projected traffic in the Design Year. The structural de-

Plans, Special Provisions and Contract Plan Reviews

sign staff could be faced with numerous revisions as well as re-application for approval of design criteria in the event that changes in the design parameters go un-noticed until the project is prepared for submittal.

Route Designation or Classification

All roadways receive a designation or classification, based on their intended function, operation or use as well as by the geometry of the facility. The terminology can vary between states, jurisdictions and agencies. Both numbers and words are often used. The numbers can refer to a federal, state, county or township system. The wording may use terms such as urban, rural, collector, distributor, arterial, primary, secondary, major, minor, principal, freeway, highway and Interstate.

If a project is to cover several locations, it is common for the designation or classification to reflect the terminology relative to a region that uses terms that differ from those used by the client. Generally the Title Sheet is the first sheet that displays the roadway designation or classification. Future reference to the roadway designation or classification can provide the information necessary to verify the suitability of a pavement to serve as a detour route for heavy traffic or to track changes in the characteristics of regional travel.

Pavement Type

While there are literally four million miles of roadways in the continental United States, only about half are paved. In various locales, a numbered route roadway could be a dirt, gravel, chip-sealed aggregate or full-depth aggregate road, but it would not necessarily be described as a paved road in the same fashion that the term would be applied to a concrete-surfaced or asphalt pavement.

Within the categories of concrete and asphalt pavements, there are a number of sub-categories for use on the Title Sheet to define a project in a word or two. An asphalt-surfaced pavement can be full depth or it can be a component of a compound pavement having a thin layer of asphalt placed over a variety of base courses. A concrete-surfaced pavement might consist of plain, jointed or reinforced concrete, all of which are different with regard to construction methods, service life and adaptability to various rehabilitation approaches.

The terms asphalt and concrete may engender differing images depending on the individual reading or hearing the term. Often, the subtleties of the pavement design will be of no interest to the driver or casual observer. The information displayed on the Title Sheet is of greater importance when referenced during a future contract, since the pavement type can immediately impact selection of construction type, pavement rehabilitation and the re-use of removed portions of the pavement for other purposes, such as recycled bituminous materials. It is necessary to use the correct terminology when labeling the pavement type in order to avoid mismatching the pavement with another type. Plan revisions to implement jointing of two different types of pavement can be avoided if the identity of the adjoining pavement is known at the beginning of the project, and is conveyed to the design staff as personnel and management changes occur.

Design Speed and Posted Speed

Some clients will require listing design speed or the posted speed for a roadway facility on the Title Sheet for quick comparison with criteria as well as for future reference during the life of the project. The design speed will govern the selection of horizontal and vertical geometry, lane width, sign information and sight distances. The posted speed limit is subject to legal implementation. The design speed applies to traffic analysis, detour selection and realignment studies.

The design speed is not necessarily interchangeable with the posted speed limit, and a clear understanding of this concept will avoid redesign of signing, traffic control, construction staging and roadside safety elements.

Plans, Special Provisions and Contract Plan Reviews

Responsible Parties

Most projects begin with planning, meetings and decisions within an agency. A project may have an elected official as a designated funding sponsor. In most instances, that sponsor would not necessarily be listed as the authorizing party on the Title Sheet. The client from whom a firm receives the assignment to prepare a set of roadway plans might be the authorized agent of the actual funding or sponsoring source, but the client may not be the ultimate responsible party. The term "responsible" does not indicate maintenance jurisdiction, permit authorization or liability. It is intended to identify the main body through which action has been taken to process a need for an improvement from the concept stage, through various alternative studies and ultimately to the preparation of contract documents including the set of drawings containing the roadway plans.

In many cases, the Title Sheet will list a hierarchy of governmental agencies, in ascending or descending order, depending on the preference of the region, locale or the client. The state and local municipality will appear, while some of the other agencies listed might not have a funding or approval role in the project, but might be the origin of the controlling specifications for the work. In this manner, the State or Commonwealth, County, Borough or Parish, city, village or municipality, and perhaps additional entities such as a township or park district, could be involved with a project, depending on the nature of the work.

Agency Approval

The Title Sheet will often provide an opportunity for a designated individual representing the authorizing agency to sign and date their approval of the set of contract plans and documents. This signature will often set in motion a sequence of events that will lead to the publication of intent to receive bids for the work. The name of the project manager or department head within the agency having jurisdiction over the preparation of the contract plans may appear, and in some instances, this person might sign the Title Sheet.

Funding Source Approval

The entity providing the majority of the funds for the project is typically mentioned in the name of the proposed improvement, using terms such as "federal-aid", "state-funded", "tax increment financed" or "motor fuel tax". In most instances, a representative of the funding agency will not sign the Title Sheet, but will have signed the appropriate forms at the conclusion of the preliminary engineering, during which the basic design parameters are established.

The authority to print and publish the plans to solicit bids appears as an expression such as "Printed by the Authority of the State". The plans become the property of the constructing agency in most cases, and are not transferable to other agencies without proper legal documentation.

Licensed Professional Seal

All work designed to serve the public good is prepared under the direct supervision of a licensed or registered professional engineer. In some cases, a project may be signed and sealed by an architect or by a Landscape Engineer. In addition, structural, electrical or architectural work will require the signature and seal of the appropriate individual who bears the liability for the safety of the public, required by law to be identified in most funding jurisdictions.

A sample set of plans can be the best guide for the layout or hierarchy of agency recognition on the Title Sheet. This will only be the case when the sample set represents similar work, similar funding conditions and a similar approval process, and is a recent product, prepared for the same client contact. Better still, it would be considered highly professional to simply ask the client if the sample set represents

Plans, Special Provisions and Contract Plan Reviews

the latest in the client's expectations. The client would not appreciate having to remind the design firm of the project location, the source of funds or the name of the client agency that authorized the work. Often this information appears in correspondence, agreements and minutes of meetings. The unnecessary expenditure of labor dollars will be avoided by preparing a sample sheet for the client's review if the assigned staff is not able to access the necessary information that is to appear on the Title Sheet. Staff changes within the client organization are as frequent as those which occur in design firms. It is not unusual for a final draft of a Title Sheet to be returned for revisions due to staff reorganization in a client agency. This can be avoided by having the client contact perform a quick review of the names listed on the Title Sheet.

Miscellaneous Information

For ease of filing, paperwork reduction, quick reference and standard practice, the Title Sheet may contain various bits of information that apply to the work or to the internal sheets themselves. In some agencies, redundancy is avoided, while in others, it is encouraged. These bits of information may need to be disseminated to the various disciplines involved in plan preparation in order to avoid having to revise things such as drawing scale, utility contacts and sheet numbers.

A sewer project might include the names and contact information for emergency services as well as a listing of the current operational agency or owner, the regulatory board members, the types of effluent in the system, the pressures under which the system operates and the types of materials that compose the existing system.

Scales

Plan drawings may be prepared in standard units of measure consisting of feet and inches, or in metric units consisting of meters and millimeters. The scale of a drawing will depend on the common practice of a discipline, and can range from a ratio of 1:5 to 1:500. Some agencies require that all scales be identified on the Title Sheet. Other agencies will require the identification of scale be displayed on each sheet.

The scales to be found on the drawings can be depicted in numerical terms or by using a bar scale. A bar scale will allow relative measurements to be scaled on a paper set of plan sheets that have undergone repeated printing and reproduction or fax transmission without introducing errors beyond an acceptable range of proximity. The bar scale can be accurate to the incremental division of units on the scale. Any further sub-division is subject to interpretation and a degree of inaccuracy.

The scales shown on the Title Sheet can be helpful if they represent the actual scales used on the drawings in the plan set. A set of infrastructure plans can include work by other disciplines such as Landscape Architects, Urban Planners, Structural and Electrical Engineers, who may by practice, utilize an expanded scale, a common scale such as 3/8:1, or who may use no scale at all. Coordination with the client is necessary to determine the preferred scale and the range of scales to be used on each project. In the event that the scales listed on the Title Sheet are not universally applicable to all drawings within a set of plans, a disclaimer may be needed. Many hours can be saved by familiarizing the design team with the content of the scale range shown on the Title Sheet.

Utility Contacts

A project does not have to extend below the surface of a roadway in order to encounter utilities. Both public and privately-owned utilities can have facilities and appurtenances at grade (a manhole cover) as well as above grade (a fire hydrant or telephone pedestal) and overhead wires, (cables or conduit) which might be impacted by construction operations. Junction boxes on pedestals and low-hanging overhead wires, which can be inadvertently struck without intent to

Plans, Special Provisions and Contract Plan Reviews

move or to adjust them, are common examples of ancillary utility involvement. Shallow buried conduits and vehicle detectors can also be impacted by unintentional operations such as advanced construction signing, vehicle parking or servicing. Utility companies are often acquired and third parties might manage their physical facilities. The coordination process that began during the concept stage may establish a primary contact for the exchange of information, locations and policies. It is not unusual for that contact to become invalidated by the time a set of roadway plans is in use for construction operations. For these and other reasons, the Title Sheet will typically provide the name or telephone number for a centralized contact that will attempt to ensure that all affected parties can be identified and have their facilities marked in the field. Often, a privately owned utility might choose not to participate in the collective identification process, in which case additional contact information may be required within the set of plans.

Striking an unidentified utility can be costly to the responsible parties and could be injurious to workers and the general public. The time invested in gathering the utility contact information may exceed the time that it takes to place the information on the Title Sheet or at another prominent location within the set of plans. Just as no single agency can be expected to know all of the potential projects which might be under development, it is also impossible for a single entity to know the status of every utility within a specific locale. A private utility can be sold, relocated, upgraded or removed during the time that a set of plans is being prepared. Repeated coordination with the utility company is the best method to obtain the latest information and confirmation of the line-work shown on a set of plans. The client may invite all known utility owners to identify themselves when the project is advertised for bids. All of the identified utilities can have representatives attend the project pre-construction meeting. To safeguard the public good and to avoid overlooking a utility and incurring the resulting damages, it is in the best interests of the client and the designer to list the utility contacts, walk the jobsite and physically verify the utility information.

Finished Product File Location

All agencies utilize a filing system of some sort from which to retrieve information from projects that will be useful in the future. Systems have evolved from hanging files, flat files, and cubby-holed rolls of prints, microfilmed, photographed and scanned sheets. The indication of the intended file location is shown on the Title Sheet for the client's use. The actual repository may change several times during the service life of the proposed improvement. The Title Sheet would be a logical point of origin for a future search of the files to obtain pertinent as-built information.

The client will indicate the current or intended filing location for the set of contract plans to be stored after the completion of design and construction. This information might be shown in a variety of ways, and no two agencies might use the same process or nomenclature.

A sample Title Sheet is shown in Figure 1. The sheet resembles the Title Sheet for a mid-sized roadway project. The Title Sheet can consist of something as minimal as a cover page containing the agency logo and a one-line description of the project. The Title Sheet can be a sheet that contains the project name and number.

The purpose for each sample contained in this text is to provide a foundation upon which to build selection criteria for information that could be presented on each of the various types of sheets. The samples are not intended to be used as a template for any sheets used by specific agencies. They are presented as a guide for the assembly of questions to ask internally or externally, to save time and labor dollars by avoiding un-necessary efforts, or to direct efforts in an organized manner.

As computer-aided drafting continues to dominate the preparation efforts, many agencies and clients have prepared cell libraries,

Plans, Special Provisions and Contract Plan Reviews

base sheet templates and sample format sheets to assist in the plan sheet creation process. Some have gone to the extent of specifying font for lettering, line-weights to be used for centerlines, object lines, existing topography and actual sizes to be used for symbols to represent most topographic features that will be encountered, from guardrail to picket fencing, from inlets to junction chambers, from marsh grass to mature trees, and from traffic signals to runway edge lights. Familiarity with the client's library resources will save labor that might need to be spent re-drawing an object. Time can also be saved by ensuring that the correct symbols for common objects are being used, since all agencies do not use the same symbols or line weights for every case and contingency. The design team's creativity and individuality might be appreciated, but it can also be costly to revise if the client does not accept it.

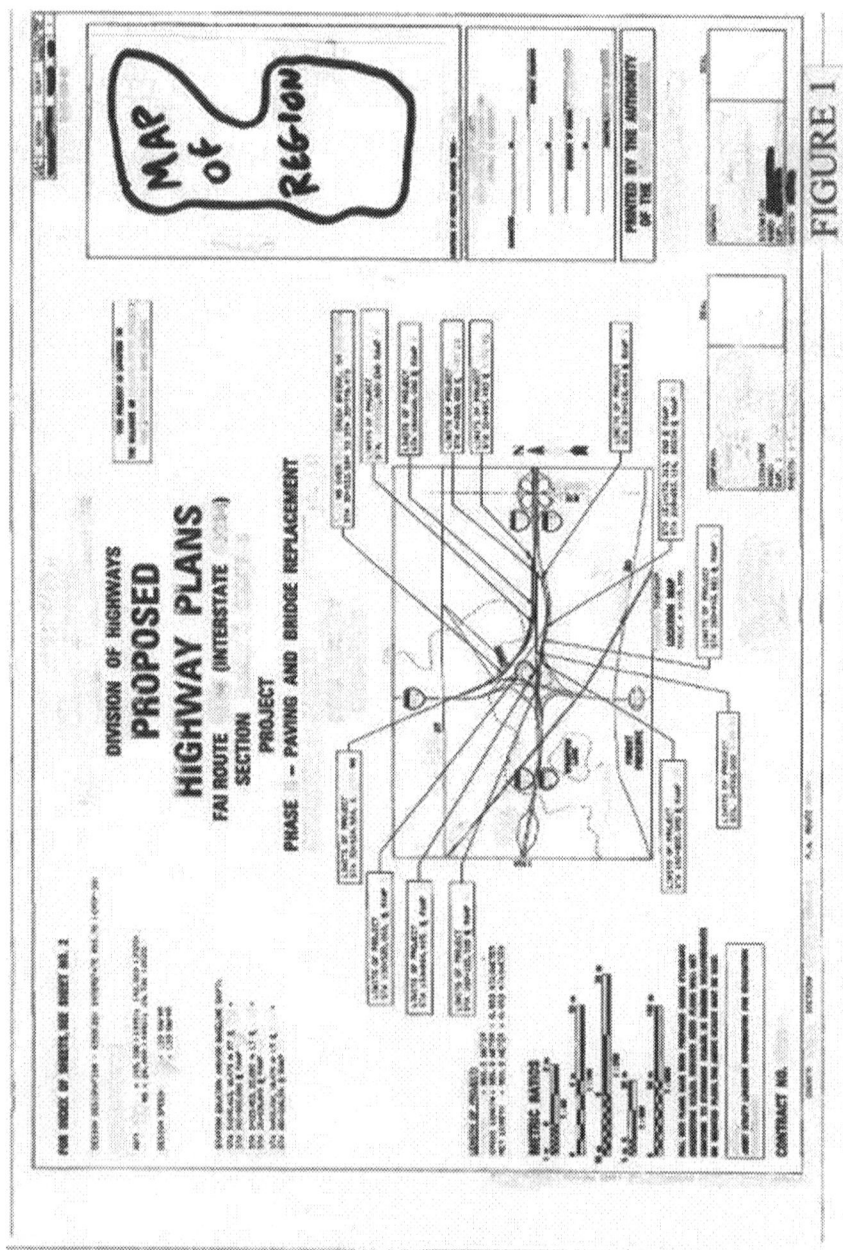

FIGURE 1

Plans, Special Provisions and Contract Plan Reviews

The Index Sheet

An Index Sheet may be as simple as a table of contents listing the names of the sheets contained in the set of plans. The Index Sheet can also be expansive and detailed, depending on the preference of the client or agency. The contents and arrangement of an Index Sheet varies from agency to agency and could simply mention the grouping of a variety of categories of sheets, such as paving and roadway plans, utility sheets, details and cross sections. An index of this type can often be small enough to fit on and be displayed on the Title Sheet. An expanded index often requires a sheet of its own to list the titles of all of the various sheets in the set of plans along with a listing of other stock agency standards and details that are referenced and may or may not be included within the plan set, depending on the client practice and reproduction cost restraints. The various other standards that are listed in the index but not included in the set of plans may need to be obtained by the contractor for use on the project. Incorrect reference may become an element of a change order, thereby requiring an assurance that the references are both accurate and up to date.

If the index requires its own Index Sheet, then it is typical to list each drawing contained or referenced in the set of plans by its full name. The order in which the sheets appear in the set of plans will vary by state, region, agency and funding source. Some clients prefer to present the sheets in logical order of operations, while others list the general informational sheets and all of the intended quantities before showing the actual work, followed by a presentation of the traffic control or above-ground work before showing the related drainage or underground work. Some agencies prefer to group the removal items together. Some clients address the erosion control or grading together with the typical sections. Some may present the removal items within the construction staging.

Given the variety of permutations and the preference for cross-referencing between sheets, it is incumbent upon the designer to have a clear understanding of the client preference in order to avoid having to re-number sheets, re-shuffle the order of presentation and revise the Index Sheet, all of which would represent additional labor that could be avoided. The use of sub-sets or groupings of sheets in disciplines as well as the use of plan stationing rather than sheet numbers for cross-referencing can save labor prior to submittal. The content of the Index Sheet, as well as the content of any sheet in the set of plans, needs to match the information listed in the title block of the sheet.

Some agencies have begun using specific naming conventions as part of their filing system. This is particularly true for those agencies that have adopted a data base system that catalogues their drawings in one of the many available project management software programs. Learning the client's preferences and their naming conventions can save labor hours, and it can also serve as a basis for a sub-set numbering system for the various groups of sheets such as lighting or landscaping. Each agency or client may have their own preferences for dates to be placed on the sheets, identifiers such as "Preliminary", "Final", "Advertised" or "Amended".

A sample Index Sheet is shown in Figure 2.

Plans, Special Provisions and Contract Plan Reviews

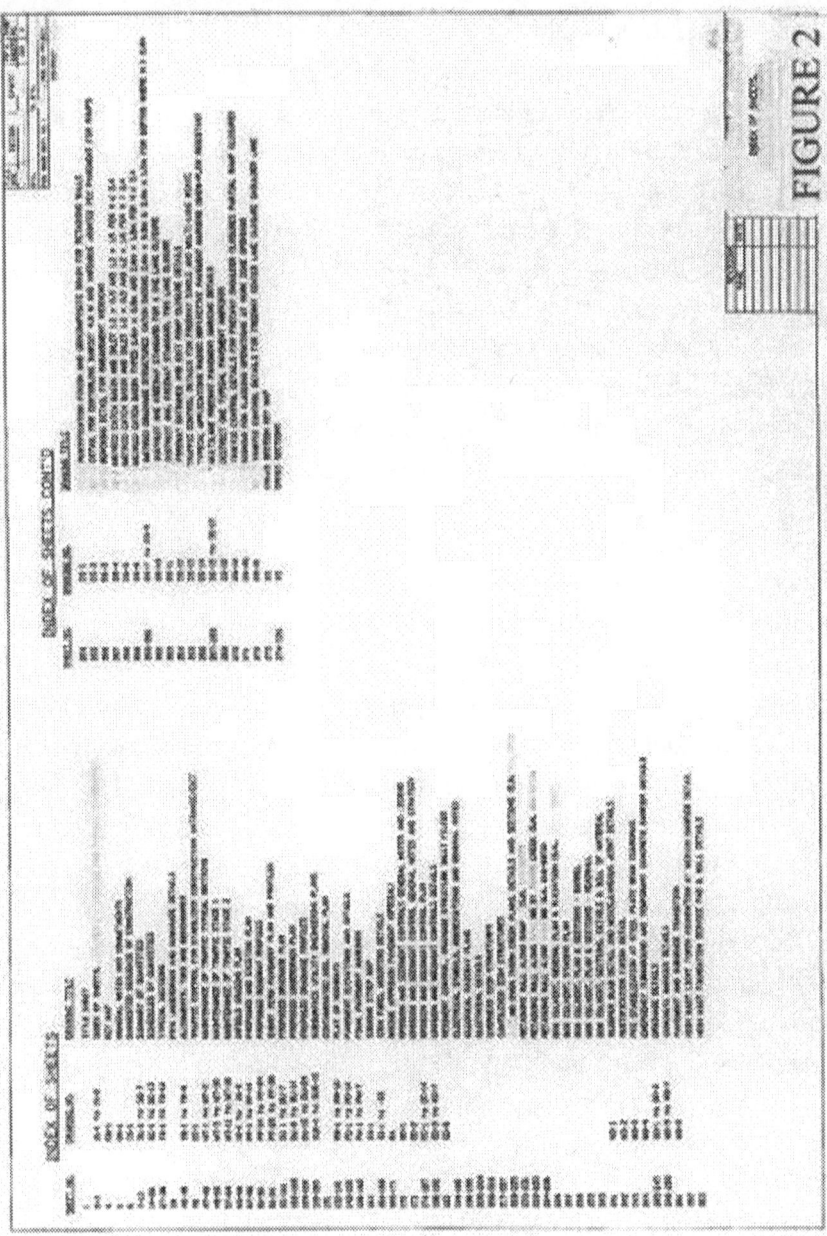

FIGURE 2

The General Notes Sheet

A full set of contract documents may include several other publications by reference. A set of infrastructure plans may require months of preparation, during which time the reference materials may be updated or superseded. The design of a project is guided or directed by specific criteria. The construction will also be controlled by Specifications, published manuals, agency guidelines, Special Provisions and regional best practices. Often, an agency's experience will dictate that it is beneficial to post specific directives or reminders in a prominent position for quick reference and to establish a hierarchy of precedence. In some cases, repetition of information found elsewhere might be discouraged. Instead, reference might be made to the preferred criteria, test methods, detour routes, work periods, utility contacts, borrow or disposal areas and unique details that might not be discovered by a cursory perusal of the infrastructure plans. Some information might be useful in obtaining bids. Additional information might alert the potential contractor to the need for special consideration of a local situation. For other agencies, redundancy is preferred in order to allow various sheets of the contract plans to be distributed to sub-contractors without printing or purchasing another set of plans.

The General Notes Sheet might serve in some jurisdictions as a location to "state the obvious". Often this procedure is used to reinforce the importance of a particular procedure that may have been the source of difficulty on a previous project. This condition makes it more important to read every General Note rather than copy a block of notes from one set of plans to the next, even if it appears to apply to similar work, since the condition that prompted the note could have been resolved long before the next set of plans is under preparation, thereby rendering the note unnecessary.

The presence of a General Note in a set of infrastructure plans prepared for an agency on one project does not automatically guarantee that the same General Note will be used on another project for the

Plans, Special Provisions and Contract Plan Reviews

same agency. A General Note in one set of plans might have a title that resembles a topic that appears to apply to a similar case. A thorough reading of each note will determine whether each is applicable. As in all cases of providing services to a client, it is more cost-effective to prepare a draft for the client's review early in the project rather than to compile a set of General Notes that will be edited at the final stages when time is critical.

One of the most common situations that occur during the construction phase of a project is often the result of a line of text in a General Note, which introduces an approval process or transfers control of a segment of construction to another individual. This typically occurs when a General Note is inserted or copied from another set of plans without a thorough reading by the project staff.

A General Note can also be the basis for a construction claim if the text of the Note contradicts the content or text of a Special Provision. Most agencies will establish the hierarchy of control for the content of the contract documents. Complications can occur when external text, such as health and safety codes or regulations, is referenced and the content of the referenced document contradicts the content of a General Note. For instance, a General Note might indicate that a sewer is to be installed in accordance with Standard Specifications. The Standard Specifications might require the involvement of a public agency, and the General Notes might indicate that all work is to meet the approval of the Engineer.

A sample General Notes Sheet is shown in Figure 3.

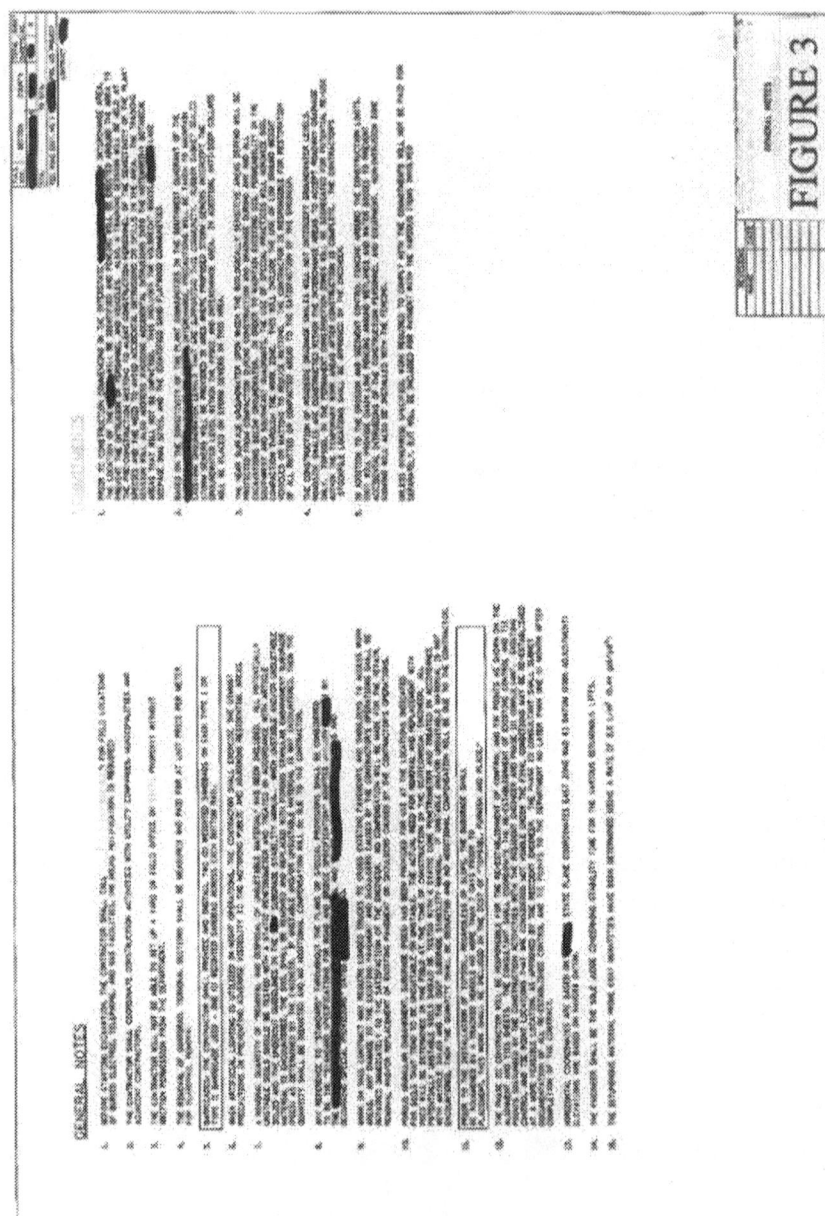

Plans, Special Provisions and Contract Plan Reviews

The Summary of Quantities Sheet

Most agencies develop a general idea of the cost of a proposed improvement during the initial stages of project identification and planning. The estimated cost is often listed in the Request for Proposals or Request for Qualifications, and is used as a guide for determining the relative costs of preliminary engineering, based on the fees paid for services on similar projects. There may be a cost-sharing element contained within an inter-agency agreement that can affect the manner in which certain items of work are compensated. The initial estimated project cost may be based on recent work or it may be based on lane-miles of pavement or it may be based on an educated guess at the amount of work to be performed. The agency or client may ask for updates on the estimated cost of the project as the work progresses. These updated estimates would be provided by the design firm, and would be generalizations based on the knowledge available at that stage of work. An updated estimate of this type might be used in a design-build scenario, but would not be sufficient for the submittal of competitive bids for the work.

In a set of contract documents and plans for an infrastructure project, the items to be constructed will often have a specific, assigned nomenclature depending upon the funding agency and funding sources. A construction material used for pavement, such as bituminous concrete, might be known as surface, macadam or asphalt in various parts of the country. The material might be measured for payment based on the weight of its component parts or the areas covered by paving. This is dependent on the agency's Standard Specifications. Sewer might be constructed using clay, metal, concrete or plastic. Lighting luminaries might be mercury or sodium vapor. The client or funding agency may assign a unique numbering system or code as well as a preferred title for each item of work to be performed. Some agencies prefer to group work items together in the order of intended construction sequencing. Other agencies list the items in the same order as the agency's Standard Specifications. Still others will insist that the coded or number of the item be used as the guide for listing the items too be constructed. In any case, the Summary of Quantities is the complete listing of all work that is to be constructed, and therefore represents all items for which a unit bid price is to be solicited. The Summary of Quantities provides a uniform definition of the work to be performed and will indicate the units of measure by which the work will be tallied.

Since the Summary of Quantities Sheet for an infrastructure project might have the pay items listed alphabetically or numerically, the Sheet can often be presented in tabular format. The Sheet could resemble a spreadsheet, it could be compiled from a database or it could be given as the actual bid sheets upon which the contractor submits a priced proposal. If the Summary of Quantities is in tabular format, it might include information such as the construction item's specific name and unique code number and the designation of a work group or construction code for tracking fund allocation. The work or pay items might have a Specialty Code to alert the bidder to a reference that is to be used, consulted or visited in order to understand a unique element of the item to be constructed. The items may be grouped by similarity, such as paving, drainage, signing, traffic control, environmental or electrical work. They may be grouped in construction stages, which can complicate the Summary and result in duplication of quantities.

As the design assignment progresses from preliminary to prefinal and on to final plan status, the client may request that the initial cost estimate be updated for funding and program planning purposes. This might require that each discipline take a close look at the plan sheets representing their work, compiling a list of general work items and applying a unit price to establish the estimated construction cost. A comparison between the initial project estimate and the interim estimate might reveal the need to use a contingency factor to account for

Plans, Special Provisions and Contract Plan Reviews

elements of the design that are not completed. Various agencies and clients might prefer that the contingency factor be reduced as design continues, until each discipline has completed its work and a draft Summary of Quantities can be compiled.

Some clients or agencies will prefer that the quantities be considered as estimates, and will label them as such, providing a column for actual or constructed quantities. Other agencies will prefer the listing to be the actual calculated quantity, but will also require a column to represent the "as-built" or constructed quantity.

Assignments such as those encountered in a design-build situation might require that a sheet be included with a listing of the anticipated items to be constructed, leaving a blank column to be filled in when the project is completed.

The tabular listing of the Summary of Quantities might be dictated by an agency's practice of publishing bid tabulations as a record-keeping device or as a tracking mechanism for identifying potential sources of confusion on the part of the bidder if a line item's bid price is seen to be outside an anticipated range. The impacts of energy and labor costs on various work items can also be obtained from the agency's records.

The completion of the Summary of Quantities leads to the preparation of the cost estimate for a project. The cost estimate can be affected by the contents of the General Notes as well as the text of plan notes and Special Provisions. For instance, if the construction of a section of curb includes the repairs to landscaped parkways and the cleaning of tracked mud on adjacent streets, the price would be different from the price for the curb construction alone. An item referenced as "included" or "incidental" does not make that item appear on the project site without the utilization of labor and equipment.

The Summary of Quantities depends on the compilation of all of the work on all of the sheets of the set of plans. It may include work that is not shown on the plan sheets, but is required based on text in

Special Provisions or Standard Specifications. For some projects, the Summary of Quantities Sheet could be compiled using the Schedules of Quantities. The content of the Summary of Quantities Sheet is dependent on a concentrated effort to read every note on every sheet in the set of plans, since some disciplines will treat certain work items as coincidental or included with another item of work. Most agencies will not include a contingency in a Summary of Quantities, while other agencies will include line items for mandatory penalties associated with "failure to perform" conditions. A precise organization of quantity calculations is often the key to avoiding any wasted effort in labor hours used in the preparation of a Summary of Quantities, since it is essential that the calculations keep pace with the design in order to ensure that the summarization of items is done one time, without having to re-calculate each item for each submittal or milestone.

    A General Note could have an impact on the Summary of Quantities if the General Note references an external document which requires additional work items in order to complete the work. Close coordination among all design team members will reduce the potential for a costly oversight, or a revision of a cost estimate, or an addendum to advise bidders of the additional work required.

A sample Summary of Quantities Sheet is shown in Figure 4.

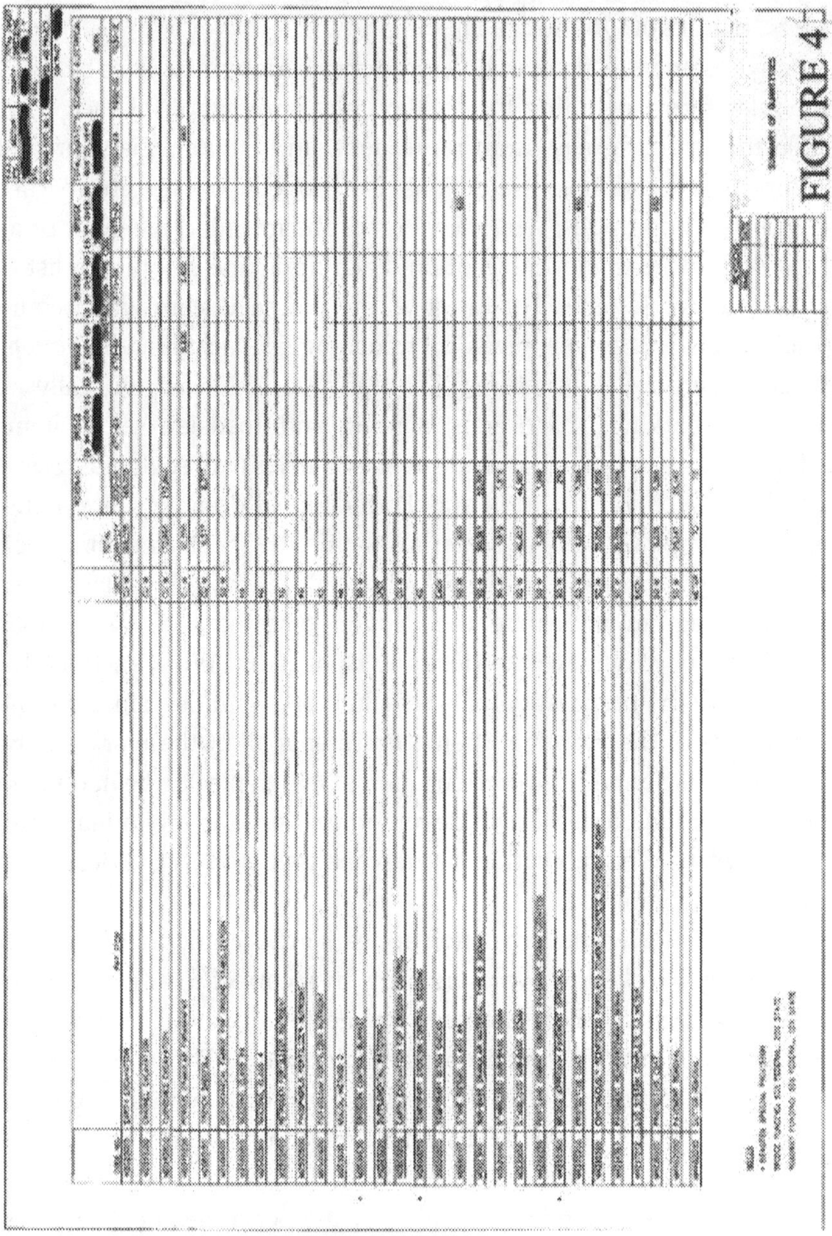

Plans, Special Provisions and Contract Plan Reviews

FIGURE 4

The Schedules of Quantities Sheet

In many instances, a client may request that various quantities be listed in tabular form, including the location and summation of each item. While this practice may seem redundant, and is often the source of numerical or location contradictions, it is nonetheless helpful to various construction trades, which is after all the intended recipient of all of the plan content and information. Each discipline compiles a list of the various work items. For instance, the drainage team will account for all sewers and culvert pipes, all trenching, all backfill and all inlets, collection and outlet structures. The traffic control team will tally all pavement markings, barricades, signing and roadside safety items such as temporary guardrail and pre-cast barrier wall segments. Some disciplines, such as Structural and Traffic Signal designers, are accustomed to compiling a Bill of Materials within the sheets depicting their work. Others, such as Landscape Architects, will provide a planting or thematic diagram indicating the desired placement of the various items in order to achieve the desired visual effect. Work such as this will simplify the preparation of a Schedule of Quantities, since the Bill of Materials or the Planting Theme represents all of the work for the respective discipline. The various items will typically be tabulated prior to each milestone of plan development, such as preliminary and pre-final plans. The tabulation can also be prepared as the design on each sheet is completed.

Repetition of work items often appears in Schedules of Quantities, and is easily checked to avoid entering an incorrect total in the Summary of Quantities. For instance, the Earthwork and Landscaping Schedules might both contain topsoil placement. The Paving Schedules and the Traffic Control Schedules might both contain aggregate for temporary driveways or construction access from adjacent unpaved areas.

Most clients recognize the value of the Schedules of Quantities. Since the compilation of quantities is an essential element of the plan

Plans, Special Provisions and Contract Plan Reviews

preparation process, the labor hours assigned or allowed for the task is viewed as a repetition of the quantity takeoff hours. Communication with the client can validate the necessity for labor hours that specifically address the preparation of the Schedules, but the effort can be questioned if the Schedules are not complete or are out of phase with the work shown on the plan sheets. The quantity totals for each item of work listed in a Schedule are intended to match the total listed in the Summary. The two totals would be expected to be the same, but in some cases, a contingency or rounding is allowed by the agency to cover a potential over-run during construction. Computerized tabulation might produce a total in the Schedules of Quantities that differs from the total that appears in the Summary of Quantities. The totals may need to be verified if the number of decimals places shown in a measurement are different. In most situations, the Summary of Quantities is taken to match the intended total amount of work to be performed. The nomenclature for the work items is intended to match the label or identification of the work shown in the Summary of Quantities, the Typical Sections and the Plan views,

Sample Schedules of Quantities Sheets are shown in Figures 5 and 6.

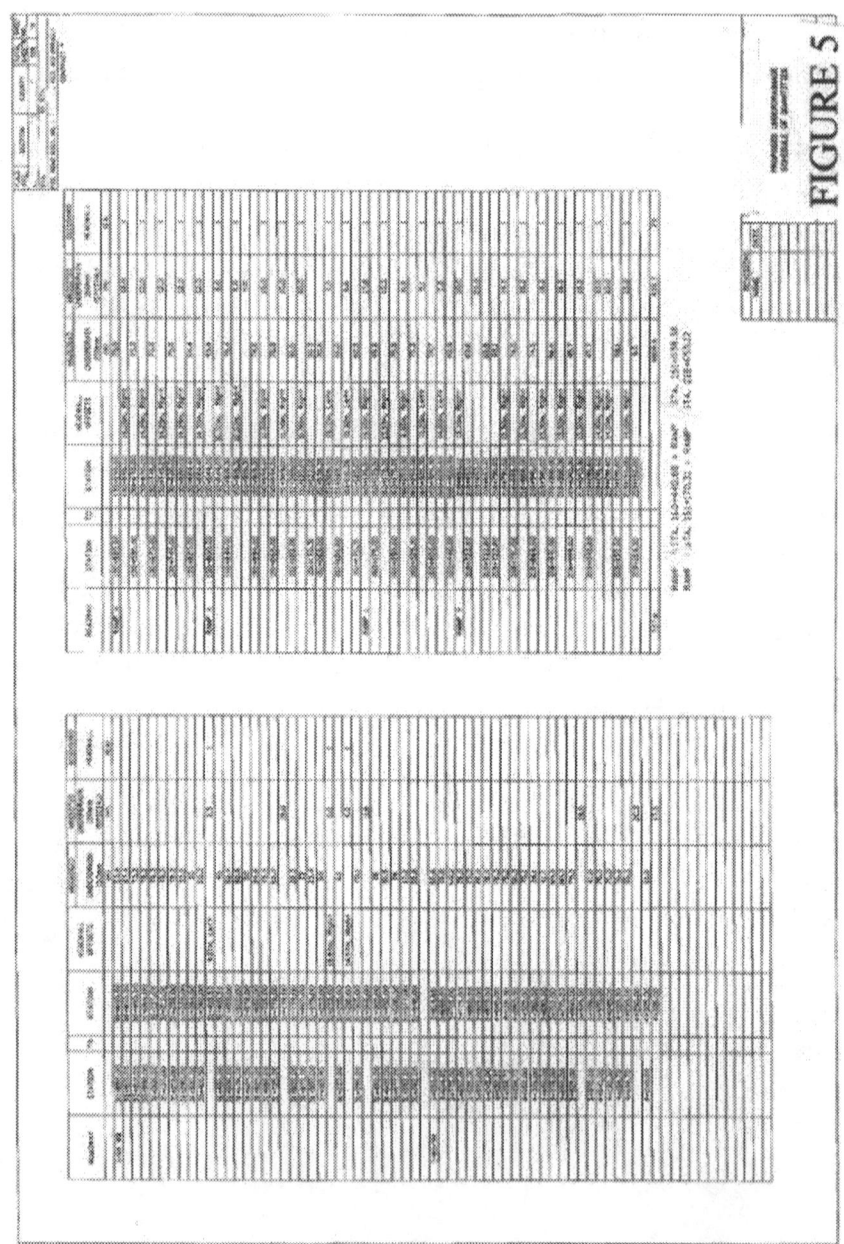

Plans, Special Provisions and Contract Plan Reviews

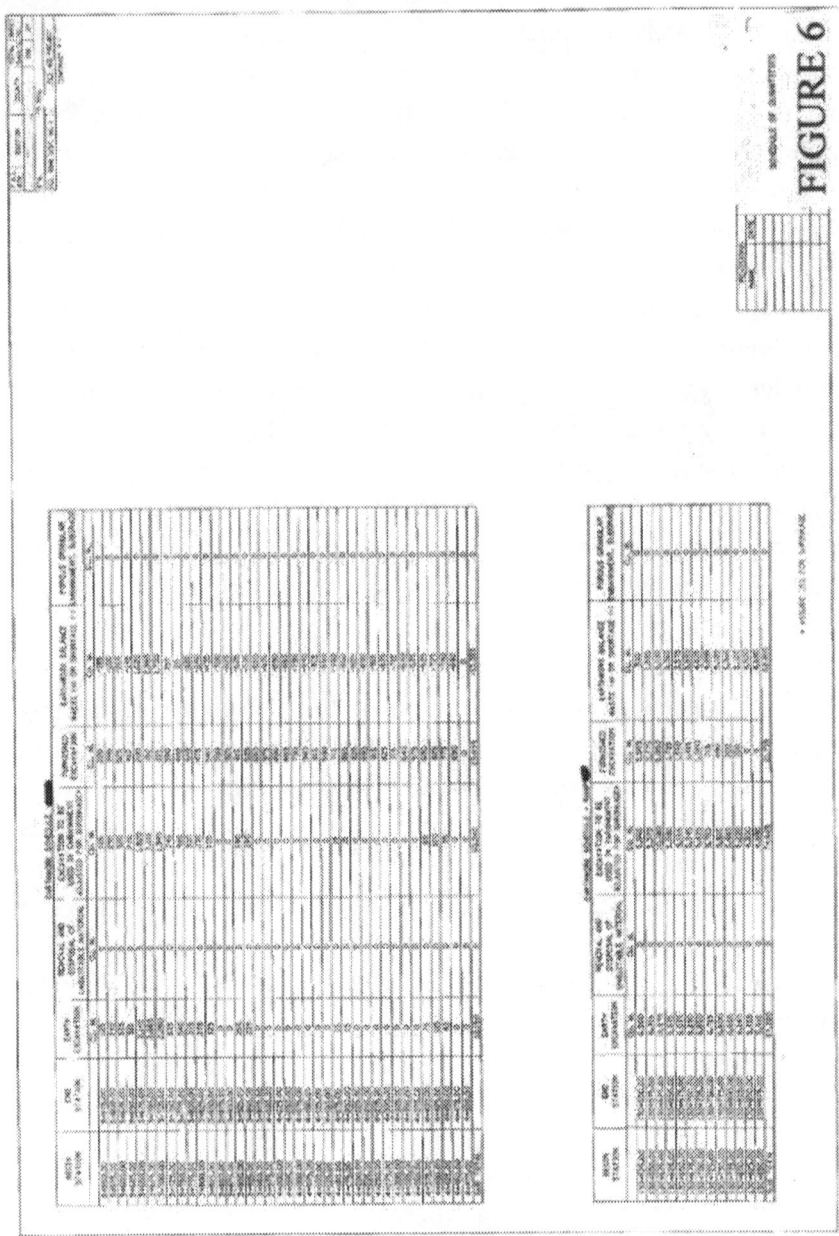

The Typical Sections Sheet

The nature of a segment of an infrastructure project can be represented by a sketch known as a Typical Section. A roadway segment, for example, can be represented by both an existing and a proposed condition. A sewer or pipeline project might be represented by a common trench section. A grading project might be represented in "typical" fashion by a section that indicates the amount of topsoil to be removed.

Any infrastructure project involving a linear component can be represented by a typical section. This applies to sidewalks, ditches, runways, jogging paths, pipelines, utility trenches, levees, berms, canals, retaining walls, curbs, medians, rails and shipping channels. The section remains "typical" as long as it is representative of the infrastructure item at the location indicated. If one component or another of the construction materials are changed, or if the shape of a ditch, the width of a parkway or type of curb changes, a different "typical" section or a note advising the extent of the difference in construction would be needed.

Typical sections are usually shown from the viewer's vantage point looking ahead, or up-station, or forward from the point of beginning. Often for ease of illustration, a typical section will be shown in "mirror-image" to reduce repetition or to reduce the number of sheets in a set of plans. A note would be provided to indicate this condition.

Some clients or agencies prefer to use directional information such as "viewed looking east" or "view is similar in both directions from mainline roadway". The individual preference of the client will dictate the need to provide this information.

A segment of roadway may be slated for rehabilitation, widening, reconstruction or complete removal. In any situation, the nature of the construction of the existing roadway is useful information for the contractor in both the bidding and construction phases of a project. Knowing what has to be removed, widened, rehabilitated or used for construction staging is essential for the submittal of a responsive bid.

Plans, Special Provisions and Contract Plan Reviews

During the preliminary design and planning phase, the nature and composition of the existing roadway segment might be based on record or as-built plans, or it might be based on a visual inspection of the roadway. The true nature of the existing roadway can only be verified by the acquisition of pavement cores, which are samples of the pavement and can be taken from several locations to verify the findings. The composition and thickness of the existing pavement will be needed in order to determine how to join the proposed roadway at the termini of the project. The existing pavement may be different at each end of a project as well as at intersecting roadways. The existing pavement may have varying widths and turn lanes, medians and segments that cross bridges or culverts. More detailed information about the existing pavement will contribute to a more specific listing of pay items and work processes required to complete the project. Elements such as jointing and paving transitions are dependent on knowledge of the existing road. Actual presentation of the sections will be directed by the client or agency. Some will prefer that the existing typical section be placed on the sheets that show the portions of pavement to be removed. Others will require separate sheets.

The proposed typical section for a roadway project can be defined in the preliminary or planning stage as an anticipated facility, or it can be part of an agency's standard pavement inventory, or it may represent a desirable feature intended to serve for a predictable future period. The Design Year and projected traffic loadings will influence the selection of the proposed pavement. In some instances, a proposed typical section can change during the development of the project, or it can be affected by organizational or political decisions as well as by an influx of new information that is adopted by the client. The proposed typical section width can vary. It can have turn lanes, widened segments, bridge or culvert omissions as well as specialized construction elements at intersections. The sections are intended to be applicable from end to end of the project or improvement. A single section might be representative of a project intended to replace a segment of roadway that does not vary in width or have any lane transitions or intersections.

On a roadway project, the Typical Section Sheets will present both the existing and proposed pavements. The coverage will match the length of the project. Placement can be top to bottom of the sheet, or bottom to top. Sections can be presented side by side, with the proposed adjacent to the existing. The Typical Sections will have each element of construction labeled, such as the pavement layers, curbing, shoulders, joints and location of profile grade line, centerline, survey or stationing control line, construction easements and right-of-way lines. The listing of construction elements might be shown on a separate sheet, or might be listed using coded pay item numbers or an alphanumeric code that is unique to a specific agency.

For a pipeline, force main or water-main project, the proposed typical section might be expressed verbally, indicating that a uniform amount of cover is to be placed on top of the installed pipe.

In any situation, the finished product could be uniform throughout the length of the improvement, or it could vary from segment to segment.

A Typical Section is a general guide that presents the intent of the project. Slight variations may occur within the segment covered by a Typical Section. Notes or references to the Cross-Sections or other sheets in the set of plans will assist in resolving any discrepancies.

The number of potential variations in the presentation of typical sections requires confirmation with the client in order to avoid re-drawing the sheets. It could take hours to compile sections, arrange them on a sheet, or re-arrange the sections to conform to the client's particular preference. Each agency or client has arrived at their preferred method of presenting information based on a history of plan development. A comparison of the plan view and cross sections is essential to ensure that the typical section represents the proposed im-

Plans, Special Provisions and Contract Plan Reviews

provement, and is not a copy of a section used on another slightly similar project. The nomenclature and labeling of each component of work that is shown in a Typical Section is intended to match the terminology used in the Summary of Quantities, the Schedules and the Plan views of the work. Sample Typical Section Sheets are shown in Figures 7, 8 and 9.

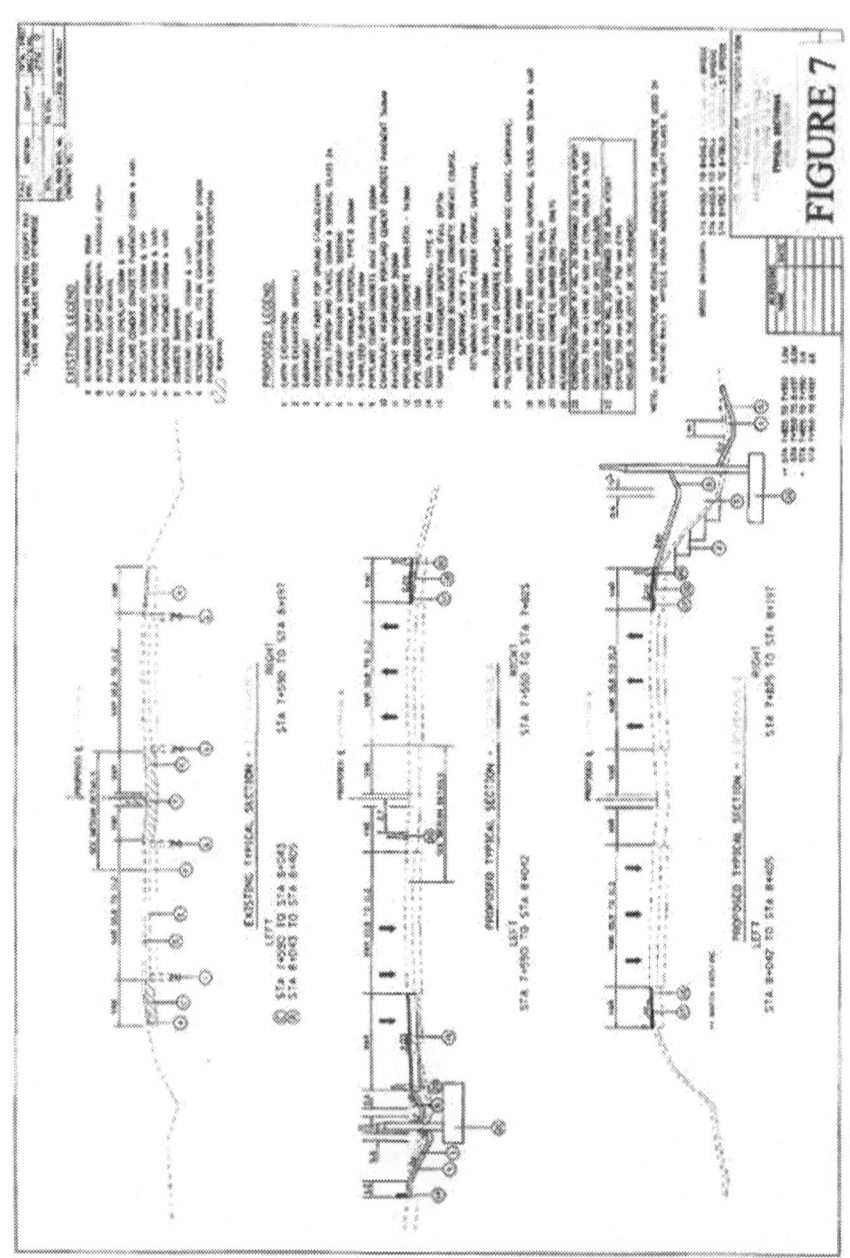

Plans, Special Provisions and Contract Plan Reviews

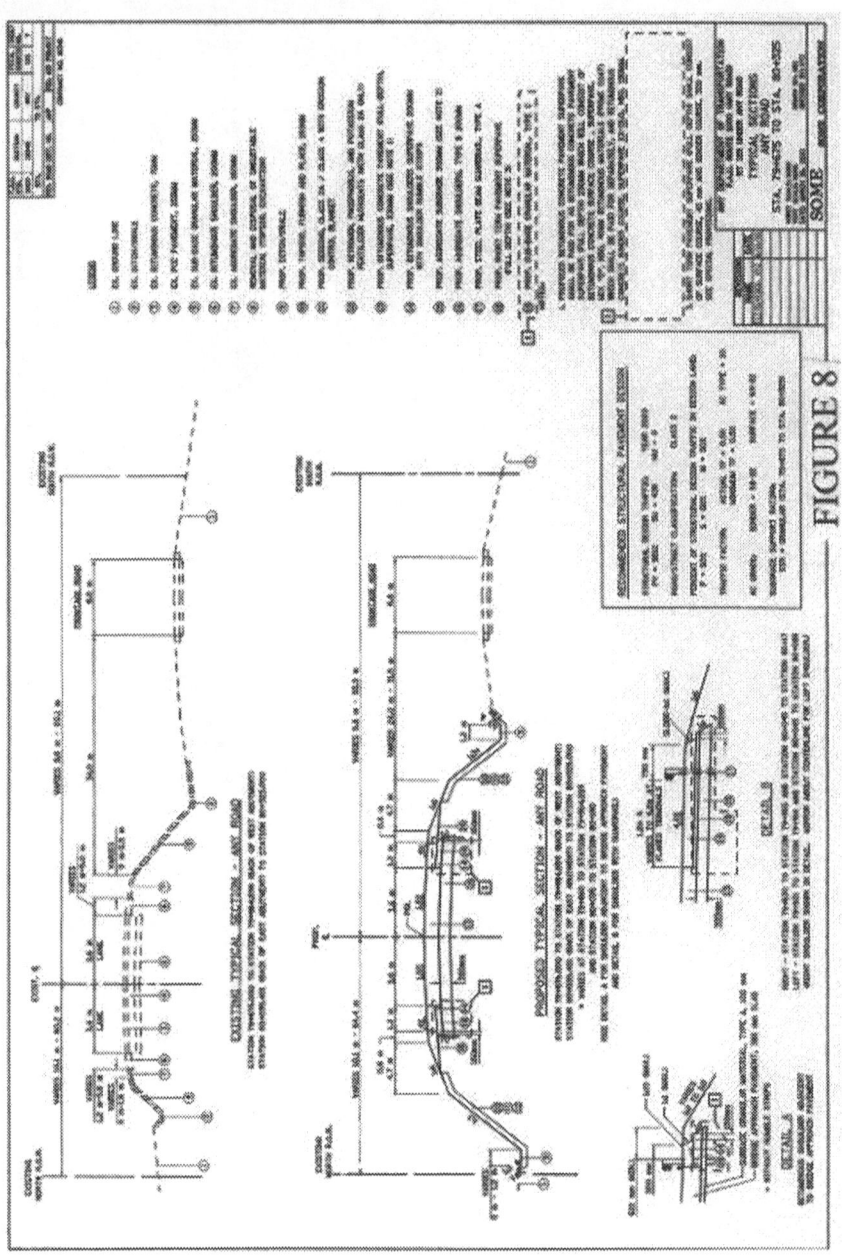

FIGURE 8

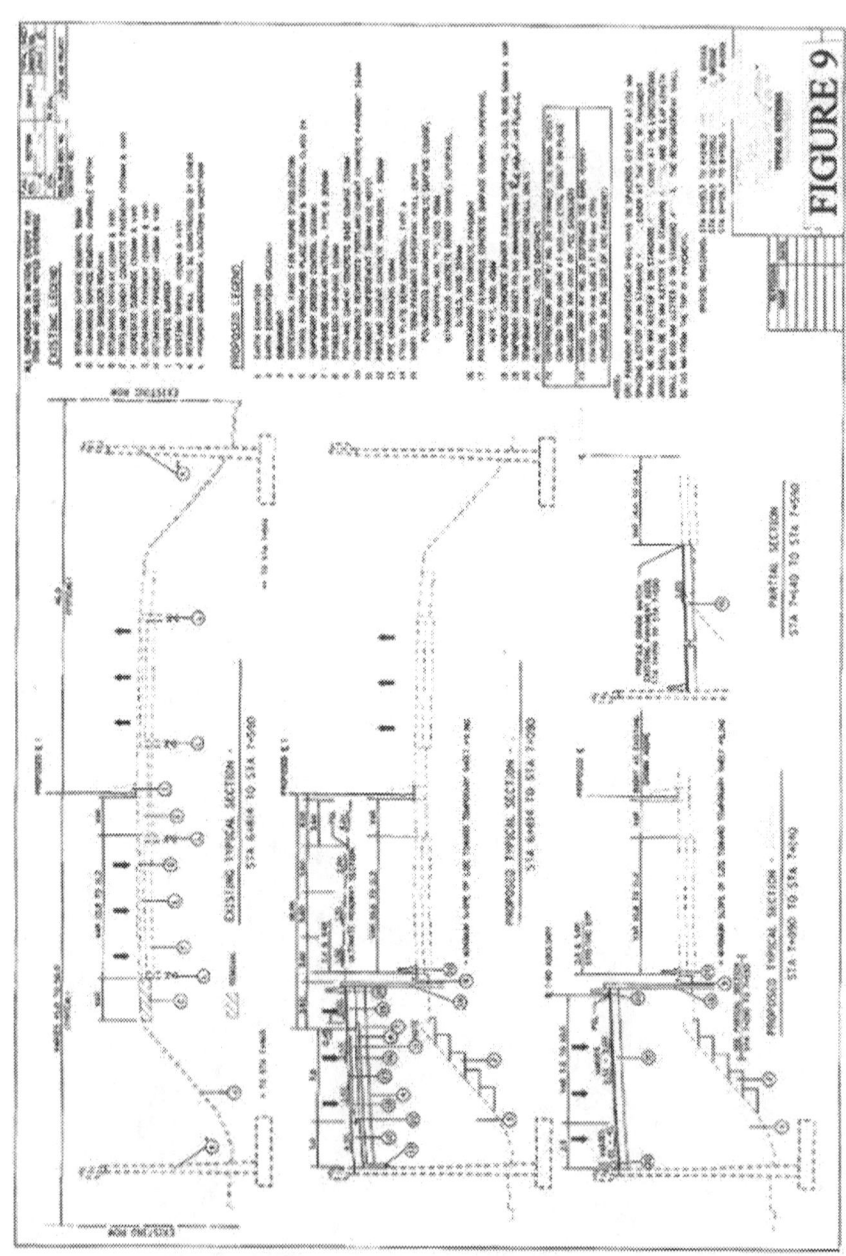

Plans, Special Provisions and Contract Plan Reviews

The Construction Layout Sheet

No matter how precisely a proposed improvement is drawn on paper or designed by software in a computer, the intended construction must be staked or laid out on the ground to provide equipment operators, laborers and skilled technicians direction for orientation and placement of the elements of the project. Some computer-aided drafting programs can identify a point in a coordinate system to three or six decimal places. The accuracy might be a component of the software used. However, the layout performed in the field might be accomplished using a string and a can of spray paint. The layout could be performed using wooden hubs driven into the ground affixed with a nail driven into the top of the hub. The designer would benefit from a day spent in the field observing the skills utilized by the layout team. The skills displayed might cause a person to question the need for design accuracies to two decimal places, but measurements from the final product will confirm that the desired outcome has been achieved.

Alignment

The concept that two points define a line has been acceptable from the earliest endeavors of construction. Defining a location along that line, as a distance from one end or the other is another concept that is taken for granted, but may differ widely in use or definition. The points may be miniscule or they may be as large as a fence post, tree, building corner or boulder. The line may have direction, relationship as in parallelism or skew from another line, or it may simply exist as the shortest distance between the two end points. The line may not in fact be tangible, since it may extend over water or through a site to be excavated. The line may originate in the field as established by topographic surveys, or it may be applied visually onto a photographic mosaic of the project site. Topography can be acquired using laser imaging performed by helicopter or satellite. A survey line might not be physically established while the topography is gathered, but it might be coordinated with the control points established for the laser operations. Stationing and geometric controls can be overlaid on the acquired topography, and the physical location of the stations can be viewed using magnification of the visual data. In the event that the visual images are not obtained at a scale sufficient to see finer detail on the ground, a field check or walk along the line can determine whether the stationing can actually be set along the line. Physical objects such as buildings, utilities, bodies of water and rock piles can be situated on a location along a proposed survey control line, which could make it extremely difficult to establish the precise location of a station point in the field. A survey or control line could be superimposed onto a stand of trees, but placement of the line in the field would be difficult, and could be further complicated if tree removal was not an option.

Geometric alignment is often shown on a single sheet, often at a reduced scale to provide a more compact visual image. The alignment is shown together with the centerlines of intersecting streets, major utilities and stream crossings, but without any additional background information such as topography. If the alignment is established by field survey, the stations would have been physically located on the ground, or offset in the event that a point was inaccessible due to water or other topographic features. If the alignment is that of a proposed location of a project, the alignment can still be shown on a single sheet, and when it is transferred to a plan sheet containing the topography, it will then show the relationship between physical objects and location of stationing or intersecting lines.

Ties

Finding the end points, or any other point in between, relies on the ability to physically locate the points with certainty in all weather or field conditions. A point is found through the use of identifiable features from which exact distances can be measured, resulting in the desired point location being established at the crossing or intersection of

Plans, Special Provisions and Contract Plan Reviews

measured arcs from the Tie. A Tie is normally set by the survey crew. It is common practice to set three or four ties for each point to be used in establishing the alignment. A Tie can be a paint mark, a chiseled mark on the lid of a drainage structure or on a curb. It can be a nail or grouping of nails in a pavement, in a utility pole or on a tree. It can be a fence post, a buried rod or a corner of a building. A Tie can serve two points, but the distinction between the two uses would be defined by the distances to the tied point. The depiction of a Tie can be photographic or drafted, depending on the survey methods used. Ground control for a project might be set years before a project is designed. It could be affected by utility work or ancillary improvements that are unforeseen by the agency requesting the proposed project. In the case of the use of objects such as trees or fences, it is not unusual for a Tie to be unrecoverable at the time that design surveys are done.

The description of a Tie often originates with the survey crew. Directions can easily be misinterpreted, such as "the southernmost corner of the north landscape timber". In the event that the directions were inadvertently reversed, a pictorial view of the Tie and the surrounding topography will clarify the intent.

Ties are shown on an Alignment and Ties sheet against the background of all relative topography, normally acquired by survey methods. The Tie could be provided with coordinates, lengthy descriptions as in the case of a foundation for a specific sign or a tree in a wooded area. The names of streets and the nature of the ground surface – gravel, shoulder, pavement or sidewalk - are required to orient the construction layout crew attempting to find the ties.

A tie can also be used to assist the layout of a proposed construction item. A tie may be given to a proposed back of curb, edge of pavement, center of construction or center of right of way. All references to a Tie are not interchangeable.

Sample Alignment and Ties Sheets are shown in Figures 10 and 11.

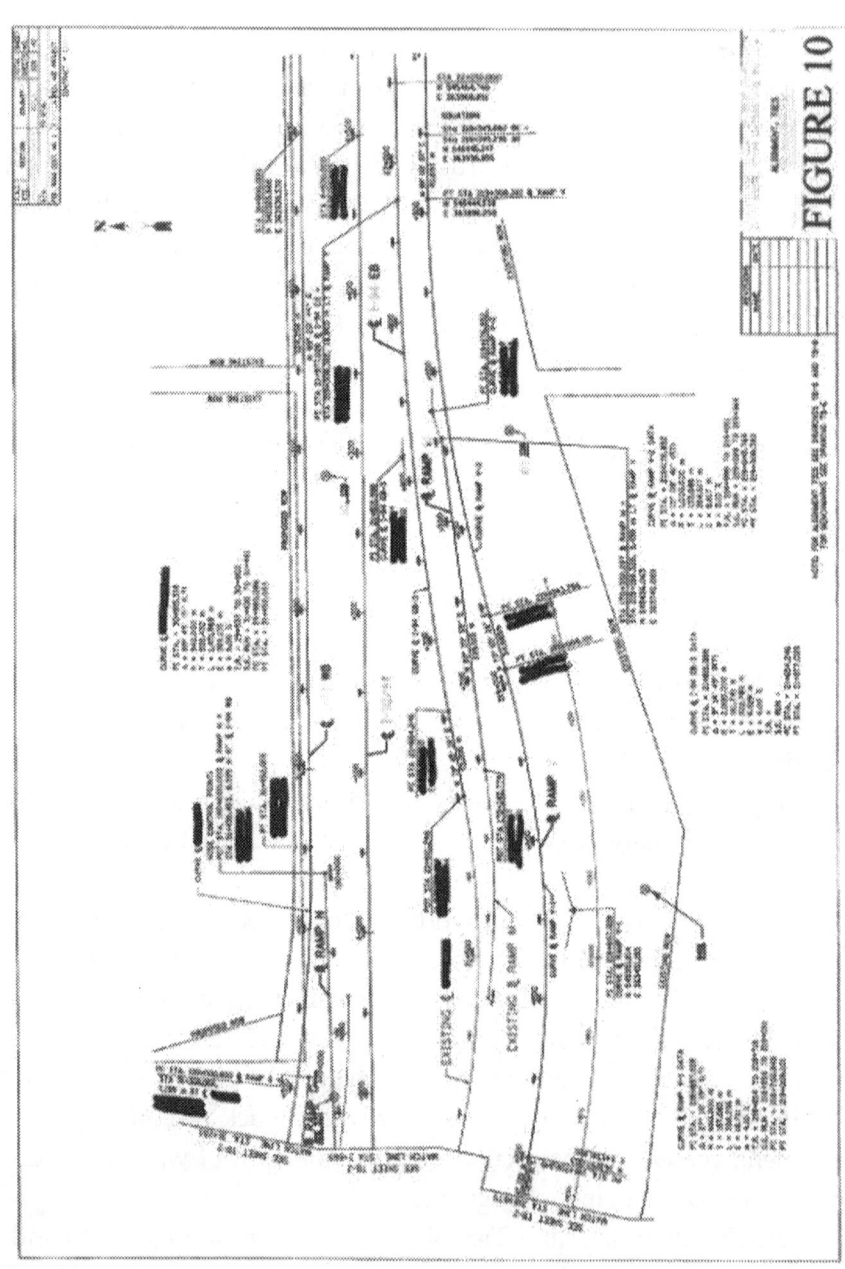

Plans, Special Provisions and Contract Plan Reviews

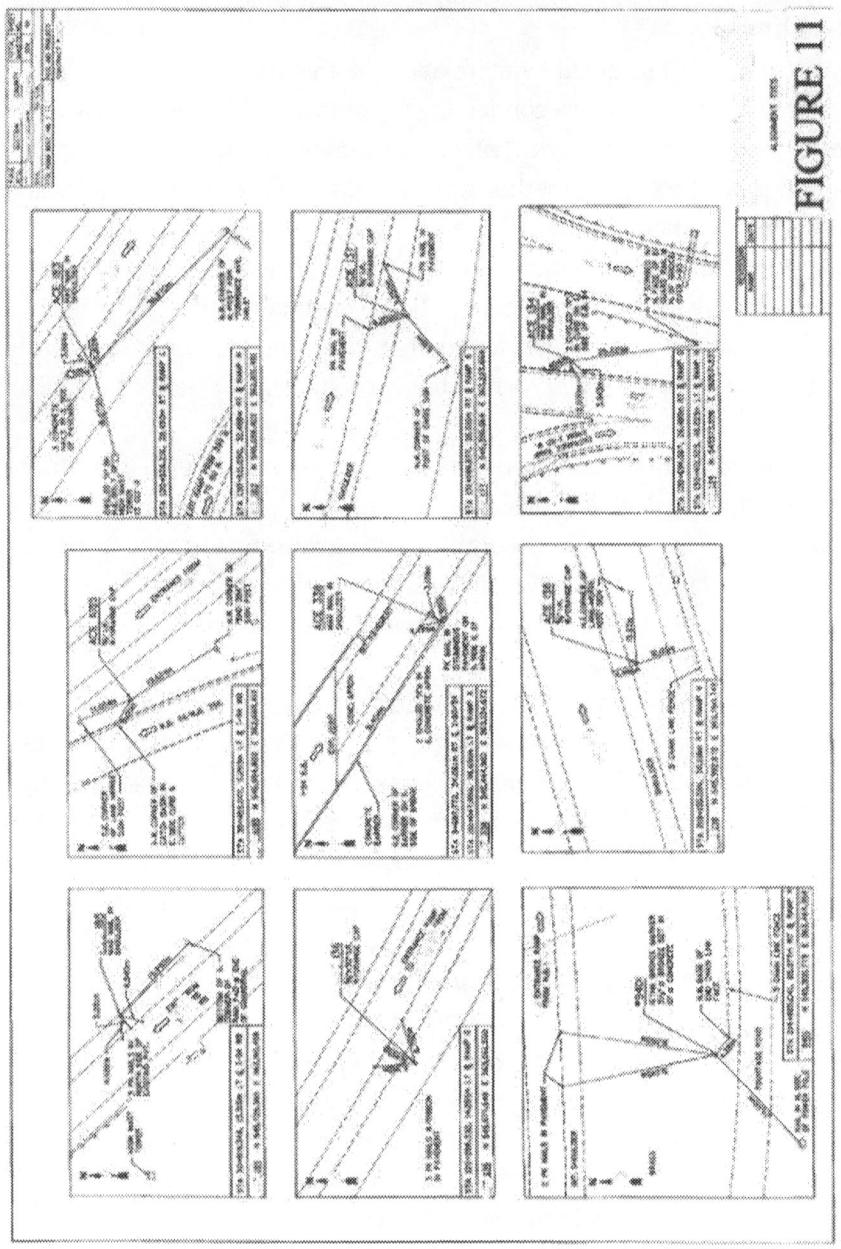

Benchmarks

A project is constructed with relation to the surrounding ground, a water level, sea level or a connecting point projected a defined distance from the end of the work that must be matched with accuracy. Depending on the survey methods, benchmarks can be established using utilities, pavement, crossed panels placed on the ground, selected topographic features or buried monuments established and maintained by the client or funding agency. Some agencies attempt to keep a record of known benchmarks so that they can be used repeatedly without the need to fund a repetition of survey services to establish new benchmarks.

The benchmark can be defined grammatically as well as numerically, including location described by address or street, a state plane coordinate system, colors, height above ground, altitude above sea level and relation to a mean surface datum. The benchmark information might be shown on the Alignment and Ties Sheet as well as on a plan view or structural drawing.

The Scale used to show the alignment might not be the same as the scale of the plan views. A quick check of the relationship of intersecting streets or other prominent features will reveal the need for further verification. The survey information gathered for ground control might differ from that used to describe the existing features of the project site. Labor can be saved by comparing the description of the ties with the underlying topography shown on the plan views. The tie has to be recoverable, so it is impractical to set a tie on a feature that is to be removed during construction. A short discussion of the scope of the project can avoid a return to the field to re-set a tie. Ties that are removed by construction operations that are required by the project can result in a fee to re-establish the tie, since the contractor might perform removal operations of a prominent feature or clear trees before setting a project control line using the ties.

Plans, Special Provisions and Contract Plan Reviews

Two points can use the same tie, with different dimensions. It could be costly to re-establish a tie for construction operations months or years after the design has been completed. A quick verification of the relative dimensions can save labor and retain confidence in the plan quality.

Clear communication is required to ensure that the description of ties and control points is clear. A survey crew might use pre-arranged codes for topographic features. These features may later prove to be different, based on new information. For instance, a forged iron manhole lid could bear the word "SEWER" when the survey crew noted its location in the field book. Upon further inspection at a later date, the object might be subsequently identified as a utility junction box instead of a sewer manhole, and the lid had been replaced by happenstance. The description of the tie might lead to confusion during construction layout, resulting in labor spent to clarify or re-define a tie. Street names, signs and colors of items used as ties can be misleading. A fire or natural disaster can alter the topography surrounding a project. A bridge or utility can be modified during the design phase. All of these situations can be remedied by a field check prior to submittal of the plans, thereby saving labor dollars and avoiding last-minute revisions.

A sample Benchmark Sheet is shown in Figure 12.

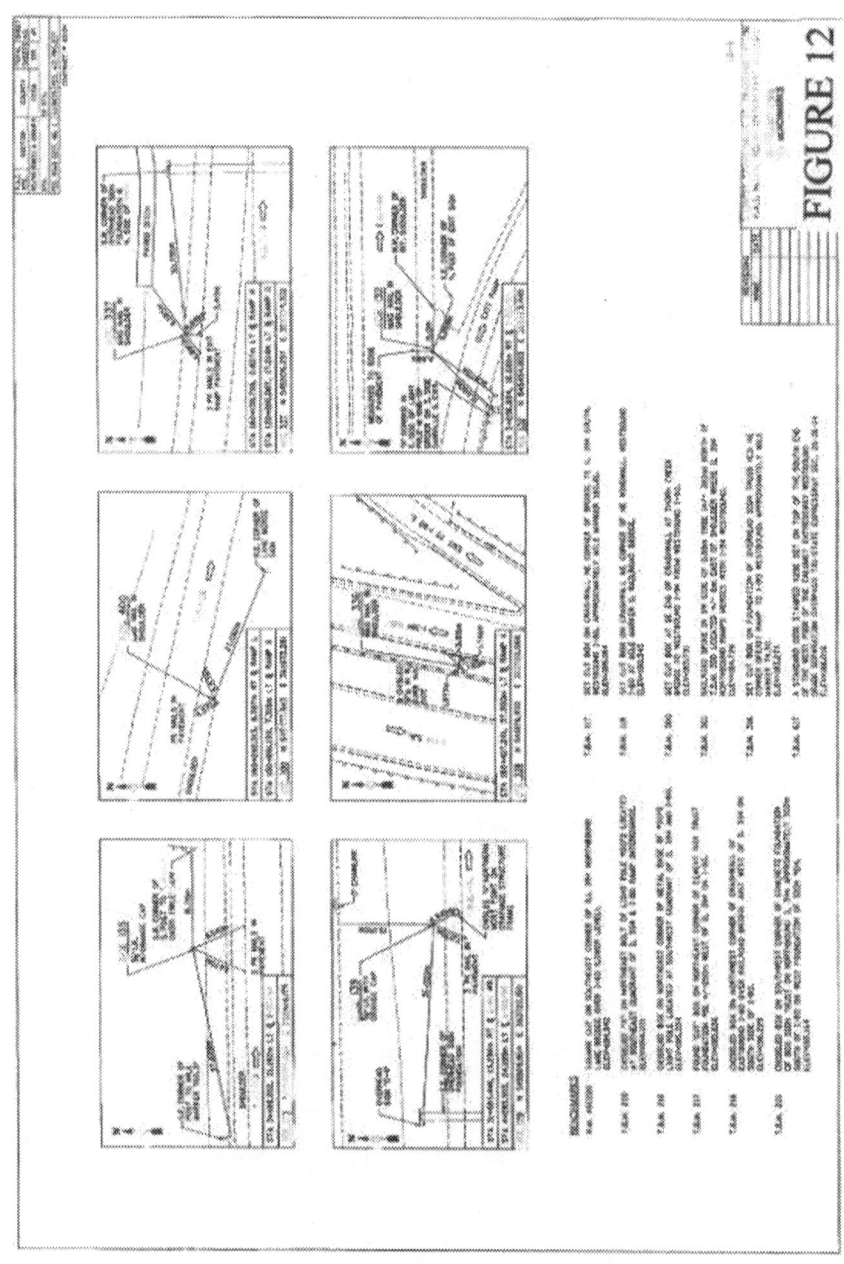

Plans, Special Provisions and Contract Plan Reviews

The Traffic Control Sheet

Construction of a project can take place by closing a road, shifting traffic to one side or another of an existing facility, using temporary pavement or a partial detour. Work can take place under traffic conditions, requiring the movement of construction vehicles within the existing traffic. While it is relatively simple to declare that the intent of the improvement is to maintain the existing traffic flow, it is inevitable that traffic might be delayed due to the construction operations, which in turn can delay the timely delivery of construction materials such as concrete and asphalt. For many clients and agencies, the traffic control and stages presented in the plans are offered as one logical sequence of operations. The successful bidder that is awarded the contract may be allowed to submit an alternate solution. Acceptance or rejection would be at the option of the awarding or funding agency. In some instances, the bidder is invited to submit their own approach to traffic control. This is at the option of local jurisdictions, and may have further legal implications regarding public safety, interpretation and intent.

Traffic control or maintenance of traffic is typically shown on sheets which display the existing project topography. The scale of the drawing is established by the client. Some prefer smaller scale drawings and symbols, while others prefer larger scales and exact detailing to avoid any misunderstanding that might need to be clarified through a legal process. The control of traffic through a construction zone requires a variety of traffic control devices, including signs and pavement markings, temporary guardrail, barrier wall, barricades and impact attenuators. The speed limit to be maintained during construction will affect the geometry and locations of the placement of traffic control devices.

Construction Sequencing or Staging

The initial configuration of traffic in a project location is sometimes referred to as the "pre-stage" condition. Sheets which show this situation will allow the bidder to ascertain how the existing traffic is handled, where access to the construction site may take place and what work is needed to prepare the site for the first stage of construction. This "pre-stage" work might include advance signing, construction of temporary pavement and modification of existing facilities such as signs, driveways, utilities and traffic signals. Presentation of the existing configuration can also aid in determining whether the work zone or project site can be accessed from within the existing traffic lanes or from an external location.

A project may have a number of stages required in order to complete all of the work required. The Construction Staging sheets typically show the configuration of the traffic lanes and the resulting work areas available in order for construction to take place. Each Construction Stage sheet would represent an end result condition rather than an interim condition. For instance, barricades and pavement markings that would need to be removed or relocated might be labeled with information describing lengths affected and dimensions required, and then these items would be shown in the desired position. The methods of achieving the relocation are left to the contractor, typically under the directive of a General Note assigning all safety provisions to the contractor. Local legal jurisdictions and maintenance operations such as accident response, roadway repairs and snow removal will prevail on each project.

Each Construction Stage normally carries the same number of lanes of traffic as the previous stage. A reduction in the number of lanes of traffic might make the construction operations easier, but the resulting negative impact on the traffic would also affect the arrival rate of construction materials to the jobsite.

The affected limits of the project and any impacted areas beyond the work limits would be shown in the sheets for each construction stage. Some clients would prefer to show all of the project area irregardless of whether there is any work, since the sheets provided

Plans, Special Provisions and Contract Plan Reviews

would allow the contractor or the client to use the sheets in the event that an alternate staging sequence is selected, or if there are unforeseen events such as weather or labor-related interruptions that could suspend work and require an interim routing of traffic through the project area.

The depiction of the final configuration of the traffic lanes can be achieved using a construction stage or by reference to the proposed pavement marking sheet. The sheet showing the final Construction Stage would also be used to address any utility work, landscaping, signing, restoration of parking and driveways, or removal of temporary pavement prior to completion of the project and transfer of maintenance of the facility back to the client.

The final activities of the traffic control work will often include the repair and restoration of all shoulders used to stage traffic, the cleanout of all drainage appurtenances that would have received runoff from tracked mud, and the removal of all temporary areas such as construction staging and accident investigation sites. This additional work could be somewhat hidden from the calculation of a cost estimate, which emphasizes the need for close coordination between all members of the design team.

Each type of infrastructure project will have different impacts on the movement of goods and services through the area. An underground utility installation might be performed with minimal impacts to the adjacent roadway, but it might have a substantial impact on pedestrian traffic. A parking lot improvement might result in the displacement of vehicles that might be forced to find temporary parking within the surrounding neighborhood. A roadway project might include a detour that unintentionally affects business traffic in locations far removed from the work zone. For these reasons, the client might have input to the project that could add a stage of construction or revise the order in which work is performed. Close coordination and communication will help in these matters. An infrastructure improvement might be met with profound objection if the project results in the loss of local business, access, routine functions such as mail delivery and garbage collection, or emergency services.

A sample Construction Sequence Sheet is shown in Figure 13. Sample Traffic Maintenance Sheets are shown in Figures 14 and 15.

Plans, Special Provisions and Contract Plan Reviews

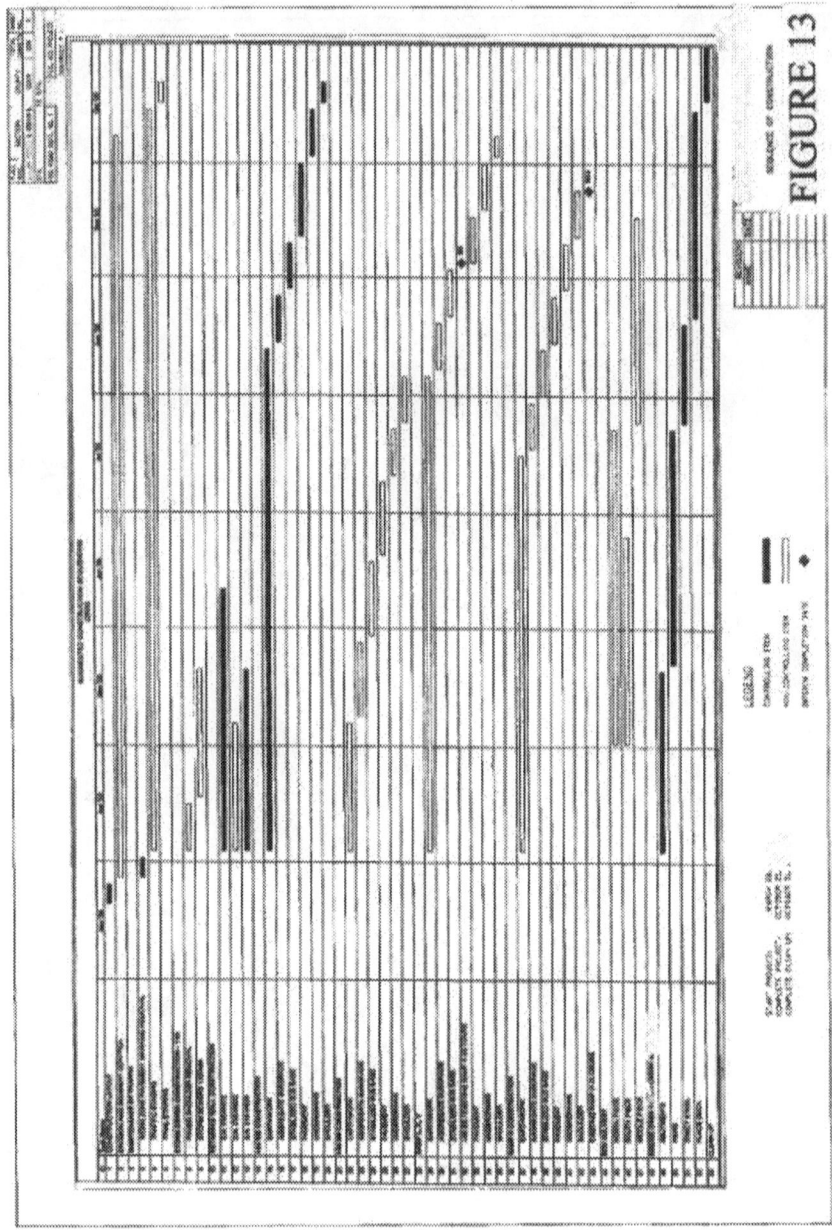

FIGURE 13

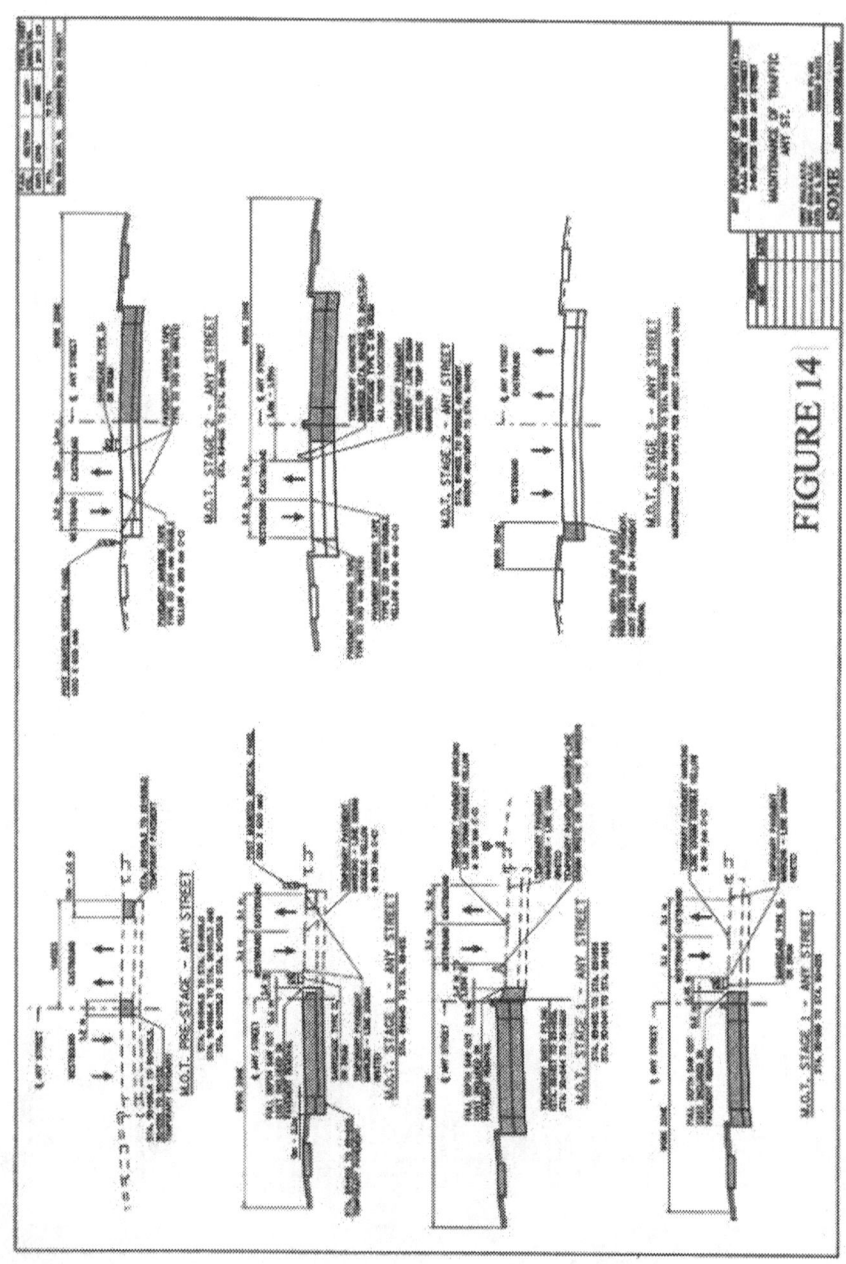

FIGURE 14

Plans, Special Provisions and Contract Plan Reviews

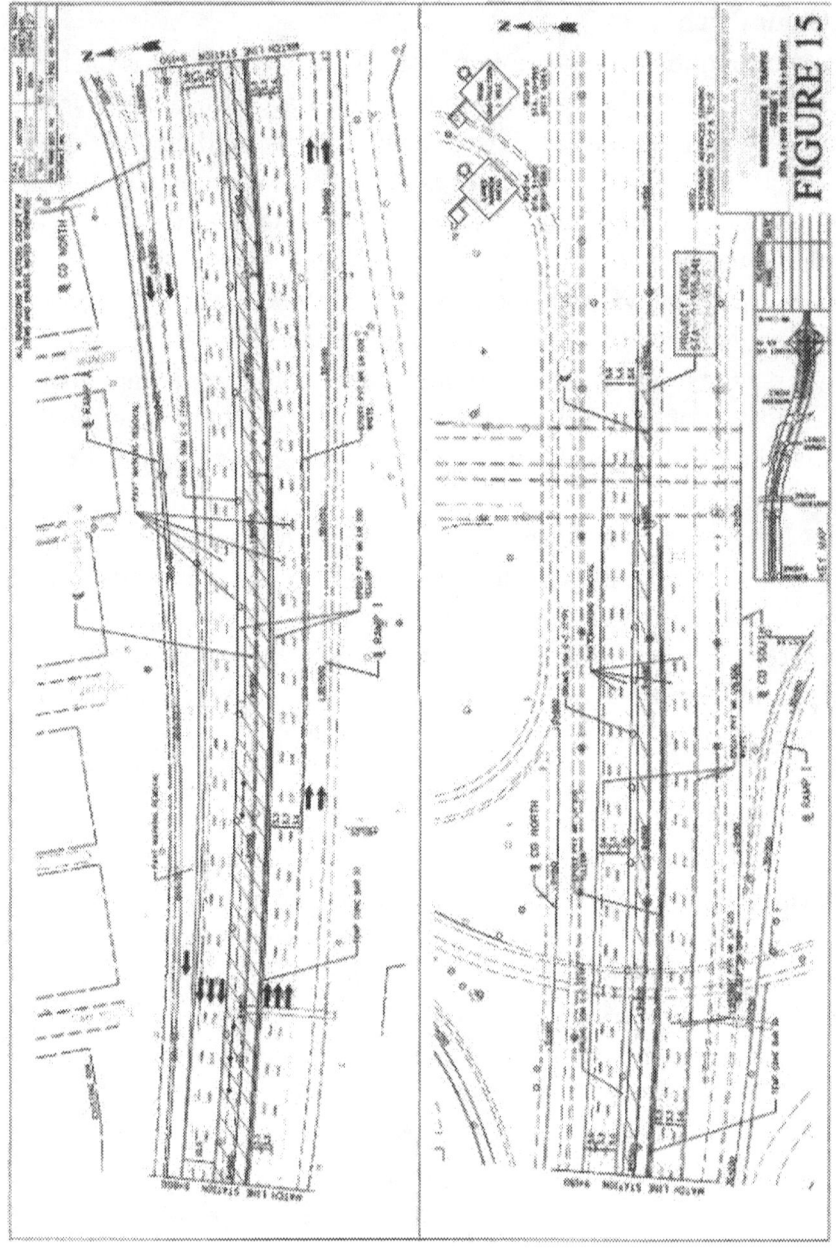

Detour Plans

Detouring traffic to allow unimpeded access to a worksite is often determined during the preliminary planning stage of a project, since a roadway may serve as a primary route for transit and emergency services. In the event that a detour is to be used, coordination and approval would be needed at various levels of local government. The affected routes might be posted as truck routes. Transit services, school buses, trash removal and emergency service routing might be affected. An unanticipated amount of truck traffic may have an adverse effect on a detour route. Parking conditions on a detour route may reduce the capacity of the detour. Traffic signals may need to be reviewed to ascertain whether any modifications or re-programming might be required.

Detour Plan sheets can be presented with full topography in order to show the exact placement of the necessary signing and turn lane modifications, or the sheets can be line diagrams of the affected street network. The extent of information required by the client to ensure approval from all involved entities will determine the nature of the Detour Plan sheet.

Construction Access

The contractor's work zone may be inaccessible from the existing traffic lanes. It may be located in an open area, surrounded by regulatory wetlands, sensitive or protected areas. Access might include crossings of railroad tracks or access might require the construction of haul roads. Placement of field offices, field laboratories, staging areas and parking of the workers' vehicles might need to be taken into account in order for the suggested construction staging to be valid.

While the first priority of a proposed improvement might be the safe conveyance of the motoring public through the work zone, the work zone dimensions need to accommodate the operations intended to be performed. The initial step in the layout of each Construction

Plans, Special Provisions and Contract Plan Reviews

Stage would be a verification that sufficient lane width is provided for the traffic lanes. Next, the placement of the traffic control devices such as barricades, barrels and pre-cast barrier wall would take place. The remaining area represents the work zone, and would need to recognize the spatial requirements of the equipment needed to perform the intended construction operations, including sufficient area for the workers to function without entering traffic lanes.

Details such as the placement of construction signs in driveways could go unnoticed if sufficient topography is not provided for the area where the sign is intended to be placed. A field visit prior to plan submittal would be less labor-intensive than a re-design or response to a construction question.

Bus stops for transit service and school routes, emergency response routes to local hospitals and fire prevention district mapping, major utility equipment access and buried pipelines are but a few of the issues that can be affected by Construction Staging, Detours and Construction Access.

A sample Construction Access Sheet is shown in Figure 16.

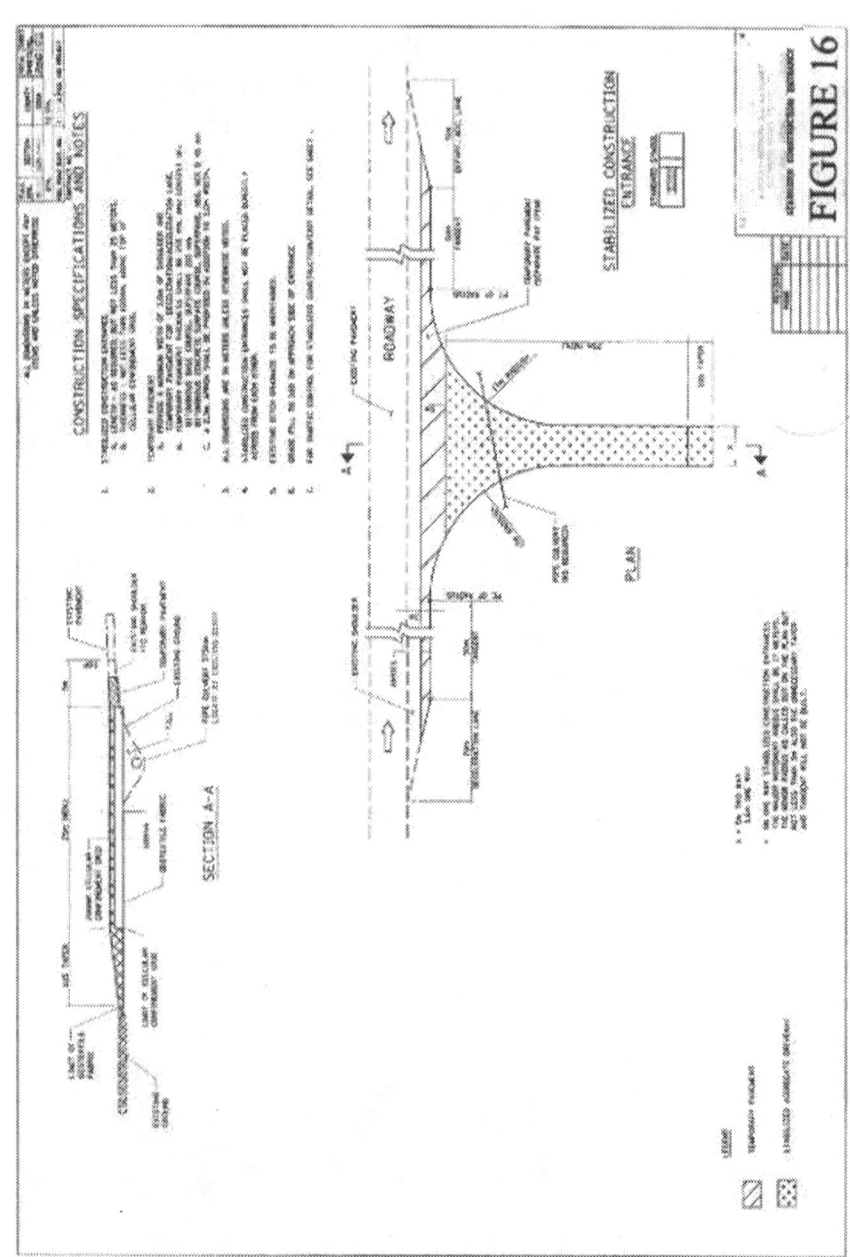

Plans, Special Provisions and Contract Plan Reviews

The Plan Sheet

A plan view can be prepared for most types of infrastructure work.

A plan view of the geometrics, alignment, dimensions and components of the existing and proposed roadway is presented for a roadway project in the Roadway Plan Sheet. The preferences of the client might favor an attempt to show both the existing and proposed views on the same sheet for direct comparison between the two conditions. The scale of the drawings or the width of the right-of-way might prevent this type of presentation.

The Roadway Plan Sheet is intended to contain the majority of the information necessary to describe the intent of the proposed improvement. This would include location data such as: a centerline, survey line, construction limits, grading limits, removal limits, station and offsets or dimensions for all physical elements to be found within the project limits. Geometric information such as curb returns, centers of driveways, corners of sidewalks, edges of pavement and match lines for intersecting pavements will typically be shown. Each line represents some item to be found or constructed, from fences and driveways, intersecting streets and medians, to curbs and shoulders. Every tree, building, gate or garden, mailbox, sandbox and park bench to be moved, replaced or left untouched will be shown.

An infrastructure project such as a canal or a sewer line can be illustrated using a plan view, similar too a roadway project. All three types of projects involve the construction of various items of work beginning at the visible surface of the ground.

Pipeline projects that are constructed far underground without using open cut or trenching can also be displayed using a plan view, since it might be desirable to avoid crossing certain types of properties with the pipeline without having an agreement with the property owner. For instance, a pipeline might cross a water-bearing aquifer or intersect a well point without intending to do so. Having a plan view that displays all topographic features will assist in avoiding complications during construction.

The location of the proposed improvements can be referenced by coordinates, offsets to existing features, distances from an established monument or control point, or by the use of stationing from a centerline, survey line, construction or control line.

Limits of a project might be defined at the beginning of paving, the start of grading, the ends of pavement marking or the extent of erosion control. The limits can be labeled in a particular manner depending on the preference of the client.

The Plan Sheet serves as the origin of many of the items shown on the Schedule of Quantities, particularly the paved items of work. The existing plan view shows the nature of the project site anticipated to be found at the beginning of construction. The proposed plan view shows the ultimate condition anticipated to be completed through the use of the various stages of construction. Mailing addresses of buildings are often provided to assist in orientation for layout of the project. Client and agency preferences will determine whether items are measured, stationed, dimensioned, or related to the various types of survey or control lines. The number of significant decimal places provided for the location and offset of a point will be unique to the particular agency and the type of work. For projects involving rough grading and a gravel road, a measurement to the nearest half-foot might suffice. Other projects involving paved items might require that coordinates be measurable to six decimal places. In most cases, the plan view will show the information necessary to tabulate the work to be performed.

Plan notes may often be included on the Plan Sheet. A plan note might simply indicate that all work is to be performed to the satisfaction of the Engineer. In some jurisdictions, the Engineer does not have the contractual authority to approve work that is performed. In other situations, approval of work is the responsibility of the department or authority that will inherit the maintenance of the constructed facility.

Plans, Special Provisions and Contract Plan Reviews

A plan note might be inserted to allow the contractor to adjust the length of a constructed item to match the field conditions prevalent at the time of construction, indicating that some activity was underway at the time of survey or topographic acquisition that prevented an accurate measurement of the location or site at which a proposed item of work is to be performed. This is often the case when aerial photography is used to acquire the topographic view for use as the plan sheet. In all cases, it is essential that the plan note not contradict the General Notes.

The project limits shown on the various plan sheets will need to match the limits shown on each type of work, as well as on the Title Sheet, the cross sections, Landscaping and the Erosion Control sheets.

A comparison of the topography used to show the Ties and the topography used to show the existing plan view will often appear to be mismatched. This could be a result of the source or methods of the topographic survey or data acquisition, and is a common source of discussion during plan reviews. The survey ties might be set prior to the acquisition of design topography, and certain elements such as trees and fences can be removed or be repainted to obscure a tie. The expenditure of last-minute labor to clarify or verify topography can be prevented by an early check of the topographic data. The inclusion of updated utility data can also affect the symbols used for items such as manholes, valve vaults and junction boxes, which are often used as ties, based on the anticipation that these items will not be moved and will represent recoverable objects that can be found during construction.

Work to be performed "By Others" will need to be clarified in order for the intended party or agency to be notified in a timely fashion, without incurring delays on the project.

A sample Roadway Plan Sheet is shown in Figure 17.

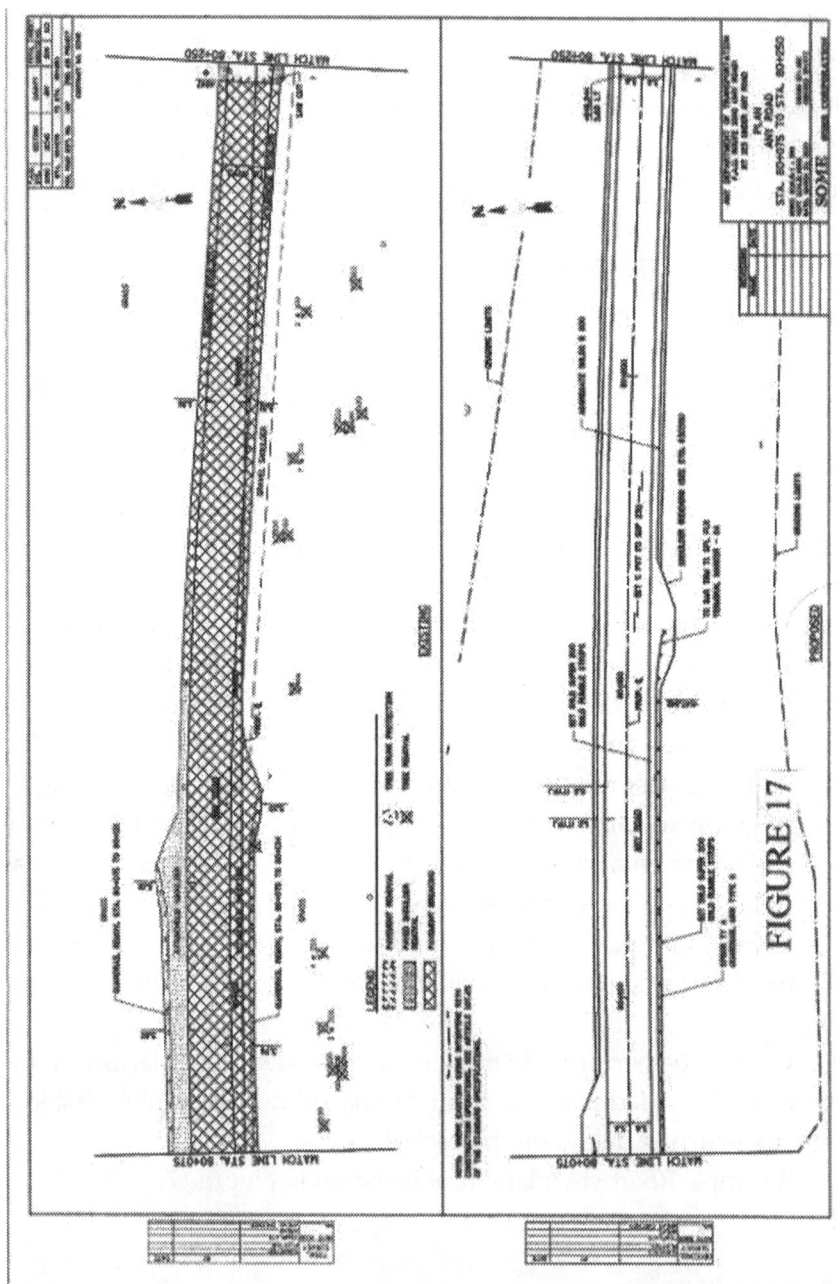

FIGURE 17

Plans, Special Provisions and Contract Plan Reviews

The Profile Sheet

In addition to the horizontal geometry presented in the plan view, a roadway or paving project will be subject to vertical design criteria, which is expressed in terms of lengths of parabolic curve and superelevation. These design elements are usually found together with the profile of the existing ground along the centerline of the improvement, on the Profile Sheet. Some agencies will request that this profile be presented on the same sheet as the Roadway Plan. Depending on the width of the project and the scale of the drawing, this request might not be possible to fulfill. Other agencies use the Profile Sheet to display a variety of information such as: the ground elevations along the right-of-way line, the profile grade line, location of unsuitable material, the location of driveways and the edge of pavement at intersections. The Profile Sheet can also be used to display ditch lines, gutter lines and sewer profiles. Bridge omissions are indicated where the profile is to be controlled by sheets contained within the grouping of structural plan sheets.

In order to ensure that the project presents a smooth transition between the existing top of pavement and the proposed paved surface, a length of existing profile is often provided beyond the project limits.

The profile of the existing ground can often cross open water, streams or channel lining such as rip-rap or broken concrete. Notation or symbols can be used to define the nature of the ground in order to ensure that a proposed item of construction matches the intended end point. A paving terminus that ends at a bridge or at an unpaved section of roadway would be constructed in a different manner than a terminus that ended at a similar paved segment of road. A ditch flowline that ends at a rip-rap section of channel might need to be revised if it is shown connecting to the top of a pile of rip-rap. A situation such as this would result in the expenditure of additional labor and could require recalculation of ditch hydraulics, re-setting of structure inverts or revisions to cross sections, grading and earthwork.

A sample Profile Sheet is shown in Figure 18.

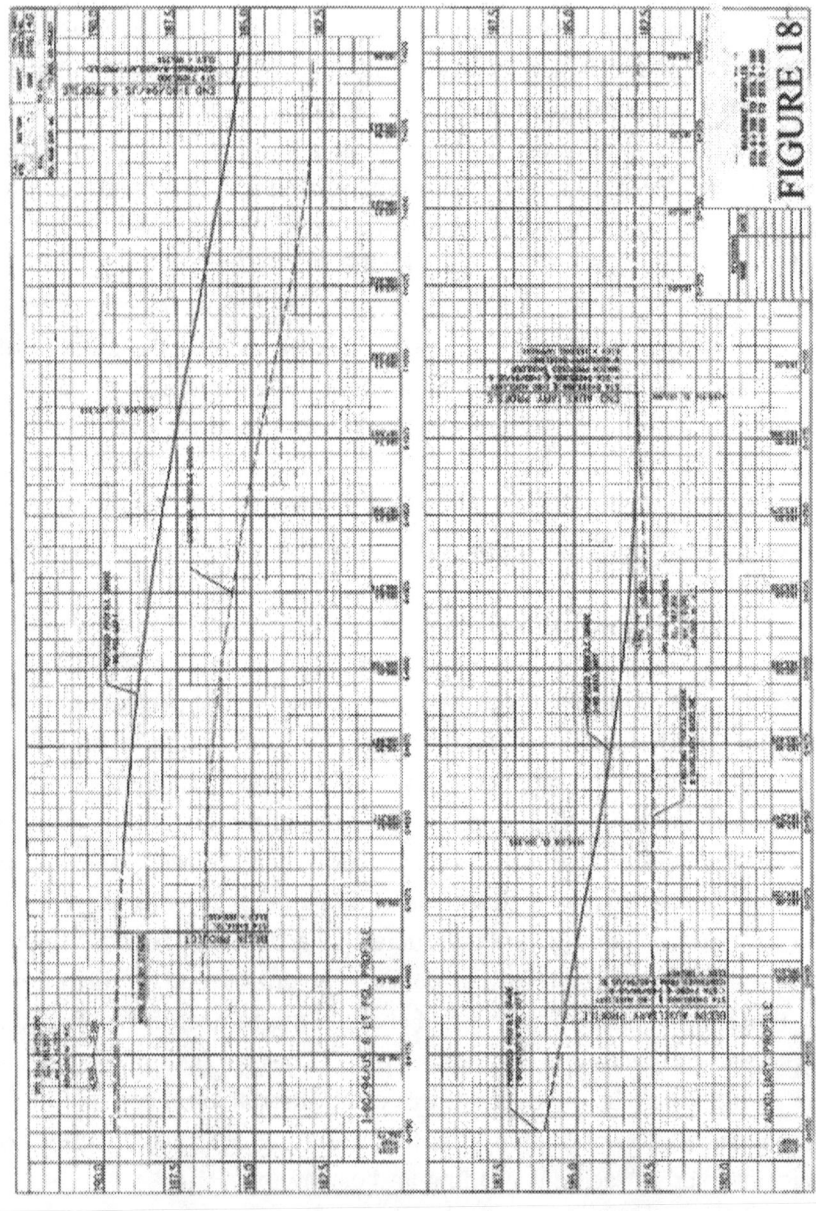

Plans, Special Provisions and Contract Plan Reviews

The Drainage Sheet

The surface runoff is collected and conveyed to the sub-surface drainage system along a paved gutter, or along a ditch. Information necessary for the construction of drainage-related items is sometimes shown on the plan view sheet. However, the extent of notation required to convey all of the data required to ensure that the intent of the designer is communicated clearly to the layout crew, the contractor and the construction inspectors often necessitates the use of a separate sheet, most commonly labeled as the Drainage Sheet.

As in the case of the roadway view, the drainage view would involve both the existing and the proposed conditions. Coverage of topography beyond the anticipated ends of the roadway improvement would be essential. The existing view can show all sewers, culverts, collection structures, ditches, swales and bodies of water that are to be affected by the construction operations. It can show grading that conveys overland flow into or out of the project site, and can also show existing underground utilities that might be impacted or might need to be protected during the construction of drainage systems and appurtenances. The proposed view would show the drainage items that were constructed, the existing items that have been relocated, connections to existing drainage systems or outfalls and the final condition of any overland flow patterns. The sheets match each consecutive sheet using stationing or reference lines similar to other plan sheets. However, since drainage work might not follow the same centerline as the roadway improvements, the topography along the route of a proposed sewer or ditch might not be the same as that for the roadway. It is not unusual for the drainage portion of a project to require separate alignment and ties, benchmarks and stationing.

Drainage design might proceed based on the typical section, the profile and a rudimentary understanding of the regional storm water conveyance systems. The project limits for drainage work may extend beyond the limits of paving or other work, since an outlet for a sewer may be located a distance away from the paving activities. This may necessitate a return to the field for additional surveys beyond those needed for the roadway improvements. The construction of the drainage work might entail the need for traffic control or staging that is different from that needed to pave.

Many clients and most design teams would prefer to have their project present an aesthetically pleasing view from the road. This would require that above-ground appurtenances such as fire hydrants, trees, signs and light poles are arranged in linear fashion along the roadside. Given the constricting nature of narrowed parkways in urban areas, often complicated by the inclusion of a sidewalk, the available horizontal area remaining for erection of appurtenances is limited. Contradicting or conflicting placement of work items, albeit unintentional, is almost inevitable if each team's input is isolated.

In order to avoid revisions to the plans during the final phase of the project, the various design teams will benefit from close coordination to ensure that a seamless presentation of the work is submitted to the client. The need for additional survey, structures, utility adjustments and construction staging might only become apparent when the design work from the various disciplines is compiled into one complete set of plans. The outlet system for the footing drains on a retaining wall or abutment might need to be addressed using a ditch or a drainage structure that would not necessarily be part of the roadway surface runoff collection system.

The intended relationship between the back of curb, the edge of pavement, the center of structure and the center of frame or lid will need to be clarified in order to avoid excessive adjustment during layout and construction.

The staging of construction of underground facilities such as drainage items, or any pipeline conveyance system, becomes critical when pavement removal or placement of embankment is involved. For instance, if a section of pavement is to be broken and seated, and if

Plans, Special Provisions and Contract Plan Reviews

a section of sewer or pipeline is to be placed in the vicinity, or under the pavement that is to be broken, the operations will need to be coordinated. If an embankment is to be built and sewer or pipeline is to be constructed in the same location, coordination will be necessary. It is situations such as these which occur unintentionally, but lead to contradictions and delays during construction. Claims may also occur if the exact sequencing shown in the plans leads to damage to the underground facility.

Activities such as pile driving, sheet wall or slurry wall construction, test strip paving and erosion control measures can also involve close coordination between several disciplines in order to avoid construction delays.

The presence of a manhole at the property line or at the limits of a proposed improvement can be an indication that excavation will encounter underground facilities that will be affected by the proposed improvement, even though such was not the intention of the project. A field visit together with a close review of the topography will avoid last-minute efforts to redesign or relocate a segment of sewer.

A sample Drainage Sheet is shown in Figure 19.

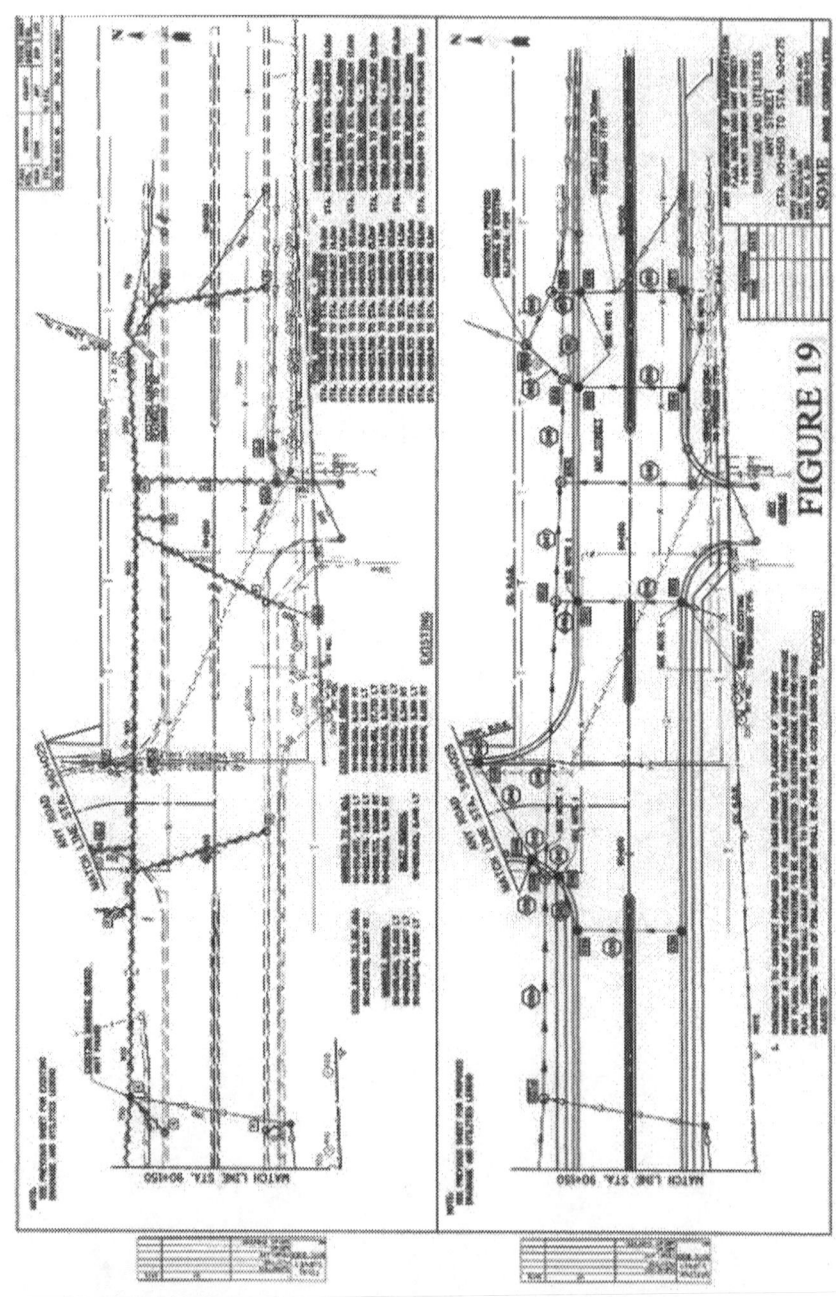

FIGURE 19

Plans, Special Provisions and Contract Plan Reviews

The Utility Relocation Sheet

A utility can have different nomenclature depending on the ownership of the facility, the service provided and the source of the product or service. For example, a municipality might provide water, gas, electric, storm and sanitary services. The ownership could be public or private. The source of the product could be generated from municipal facilities. In this instance, it would not be unusual for the municipality to label all of its conveyance facilities as "utilities". In some locales, each commodity is provided by a separate entity, and the facilities or services are also known as "utilities". In the case of a combined sanitary and storm water system, the sewers and collection structures could be considered as part of the drainage system. The irrigation system for street-side planters might be connected to the water-main, but could be considered to be a utility. In every case, one client's practices will not always be the same as the neighboring client.

Projects can affect the existing surface as well as the area below grade. A roadway widening project can minimize the amount of accessible areas outside of the paved portion of the right-of-way, forcing a utility to enter into an agreement to occupy and access portions of property that are not located within the public land. The utility would be shown on the existing view as being relocated by others, and might not be shown on the proposed view, unless the utility was still in place at the time that the plans are completed and ready to be submitted to the client.

The nature or identity of a utility can appear to change as a project progresses, based on the information available. During the preliminary or programming phase, the existence of a utility might be established during a short-duration site visit or a consultation of the latest written information obtainable. The presence of an above-grade frame and lid could indicate the presence of a facility below grade. In some instances, a series of circumstantial events might lead to the need to revise the plans or perform design revisions at the last stages prior to submittal.

For instance, the above-grade frame could be fitted with a lid which might contain the word "water", but the lid could have been switched with a lid from a storm sewer system, if the original lid had somehow been removed and had to be replaced in an expedient manner. The project survey crew might open the lid and discover that the underground facility is filled with debris but effuses an odor similar to a sanitary sewer system. Preliminary plans could be sent to utility companies in the area without receiving a response from anyone regarding a water system. The design team might feel that the frame and lid aligns with a force main known to pass beneath the area in the same vicinity. Local safety guidelines might prohibit the physical entry of any person into the underground portion in an attempt to clarify the nature of the facility. The plans could conceivably reach the hands of the contractor, and during some excavation operation in the vicinity of the subject lid, a long-forgotten telephone conduit that once belonged to a company that was sold and re-sold and is currently in bankruptcy proceedings is cut, disrupting the signal, and resulting in a costly repair. While there is no way to foresee all possibilities, or to know the history of interaction with a facility, the need for communication and questioning of information is always present. The varying information described above could result in the production of plans which contained misinformation, albeit unintentional, but the resolution could require extensive labor to correct the situation.

Utilities are also shown on Figure 19.

The Grading Sheet

The topography of a project site can be defined by lines and symbols that represent the above-ground or at-grade features, as well as by lines which represent the changes in elevation at specified intervals. In some situations, presenting all of the lines and symbols and associated nomenclature on one plan view would make a drawing appear cluttered and could be illegible if the drawing were reproduced at a small-

Plans, Special Provisions and Contract Plan Reviews

er scale. To avoid this situation, as well as to illustrate how a project matches the surrounding area, a Grading Sheet is used. The lines representing elevations are known as contours, and can be presented at any desired increment, from inches to feet. A one or two foot interval is most common. The elevations of the contours are labeled as frequently as is needed in order to communicate the information. Elevations for isolated contours will be needed to allow correct communication of the data.

For most situations, contour lines will not make sharp turns. The exception is a ditch flow line or shaped embankment. Contours at ditch bottoms and at abrupt changes in elevation will tend to be spaced closer together, and can become illegible in situations where steep slopes are involved.

In most cases, the proposed contours of a project site are presented, extending throughout the improvement area, and meeting the existing contours at the construction limits. Proposed contours would meet existing contours on tangent, or at the same curvature.

The Grading Sheet will clearly illustrate abrupt changes in elevation at the project limits. This will be of particular interest to the client as well as to the designer in order to assess drainage patterns, the need for grading transitions and the need to extend the construction limits or to provide structural elements such as retaining walls to prevent unacceptable side-slopes. The grading of a project can be reviewed using the cross-sections, or by incorporating the top of ground data from the topographic surveys. The grading can extend across paved areas to check for abrupt changes, and can be used to ensure that drainage swales, ditches and overland flow patterns are preserved.

A sample Grading Sheet is shown in Figure 20.

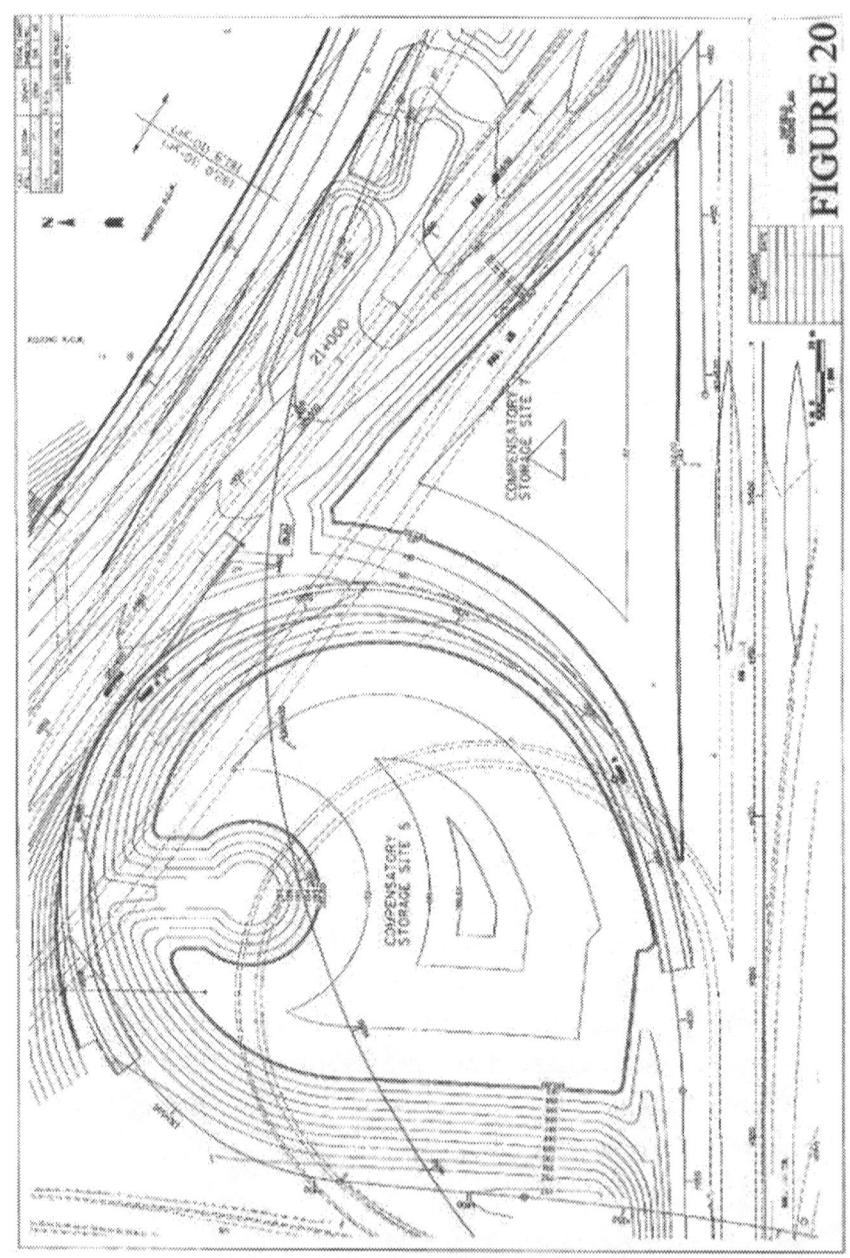
FIGURE 20

Plans, Special Provisions and Contract Plan Reviews

The Cross-Section Sheet

A cross-section represents a vertical plane passing through a project. It shows the existing ground surface, and can be supplemented with both above-ground and underground information including: right-of-way locations, paved areas, ditch flow lines, soil characteristics and utilities. A cross-section is provided at various intervals along the project survey line or centerline, depending on agency requirements and the nature of the project. Each section is unique, since the surface of the ground varies from one location to the next throughout the length of a project.

The cross-sections can be developed from field surveys, electronic measuring systems, computer-aided drafting software or topographic mapping sources. They are typically "cut" perpendicular to the centerline or other control line, and can be "cut" on a skew at structures or at intersecting roadways. In order to provide an indication of the existing conditions immediately prior to and beyond the project limits, it is standard practice with some agencies to show one or two cross-sections before and after the sections representing the ground within the improvement limits.

Cross-sections were originally devised as a means for measuring the excavation and placement of material on a project. They were shown at uniform intervals from end to end of a project. Additional sections were provided at the high and low points of a proposed profile. Each section would show the intended final grading condition super-imposed onto the existing ground condition, thereby allowing a measurement in square feet of the excavation or embankment operations that were to be conducted at that location. Calculation of volumes was obtained from the average of two consecutive sections multiplied by the distance between the sections. This would be termed as the "average end area method", Accuracy of earthwork computations would be dependent on the interval of the cross-section spacing, since the ground surface may vary greatly between intervals that cover hundreds of feet. The contents of the cross-sections were modified through the years to include pavement and soil information in order to separate the various types of material that might be encountered during removal and earthwork operations. Further iterations by some agencies required the inclusion of subsurface utilities, storm sewers and eventually some above-ground features were required. Cross-sections have been shown with trees, fences, power poles, guardrail, water surfaces, debris piles, sign foundations and bus stop benches. The information might be useful in some situations to ensure that all appurtenances are taken into account. The primary use of any cross-section remains unchanged – that is, the sections are used for calculation of earthwork quantities.

A review of the cross-sections at the termini of a project will indicate whether all work matches the existing ground. Often the pavement typical section will need to be modified with paving transitions in order to meet the existing paved surface from edge-to-edge of roadway. Curbing, shoulders, sidewalk, ditches or grading transitions can be checked in similar fashion. It therefore might be necessary to check the cross-sections at various times during the project.

A sample Cross-Section Sheet is shown in Figure 21.

Plans, Special Provisions and Contract Plan Reviews

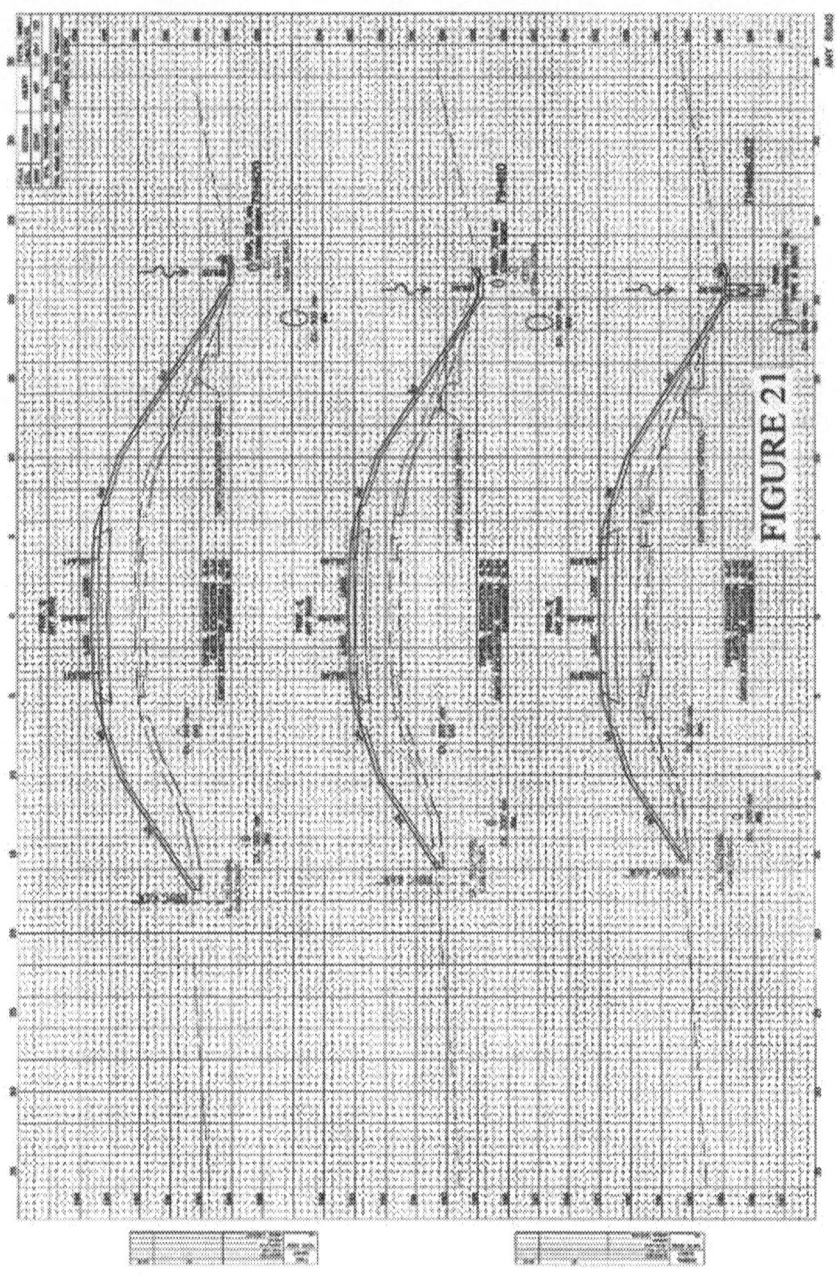

FIGURE 21

The Construction Detail Sheet

Many agencies, municipalities and private clients have lists of standardized drawings that are to be used as a control for the construction of items such as pavement joints, roadside appurtenances and structural features. The list could include driveways, drainage structures, fence, ornamental lighting, and urban enhancement such as benches, planters and shelters. For some projects, the standardized drawing might not be applicable in all situations. This would require the preparation of a drawing that shows the particular elements of an item that differ from the standardized drawing. This could be different dimensions, different materials or a completely revised design that is preferable to the standard. For some situations, a detail might be based on literature or photos of a new product that is available and suitable for a project. Other situations require that the intent of the designer be presented in a sketch to serve as a guide for the construction of a special case that has not been encountered in previous projects.

Many agencies that have a library of standardized drawings would prefer that their designs be used on their projects, and not be considered to be interchangeable in all conditions. Labor and design time can be preserved based on a discussion with the client regarding the use of standards from other agencies.

For details prepared by a designer, the center point or a designated corner of an object would need to be identified in order to perform construction layout.

A sample Construction Detail Sheet is shown in Figure 22.

Plans, Special Provisions and Contract Plan Reviews

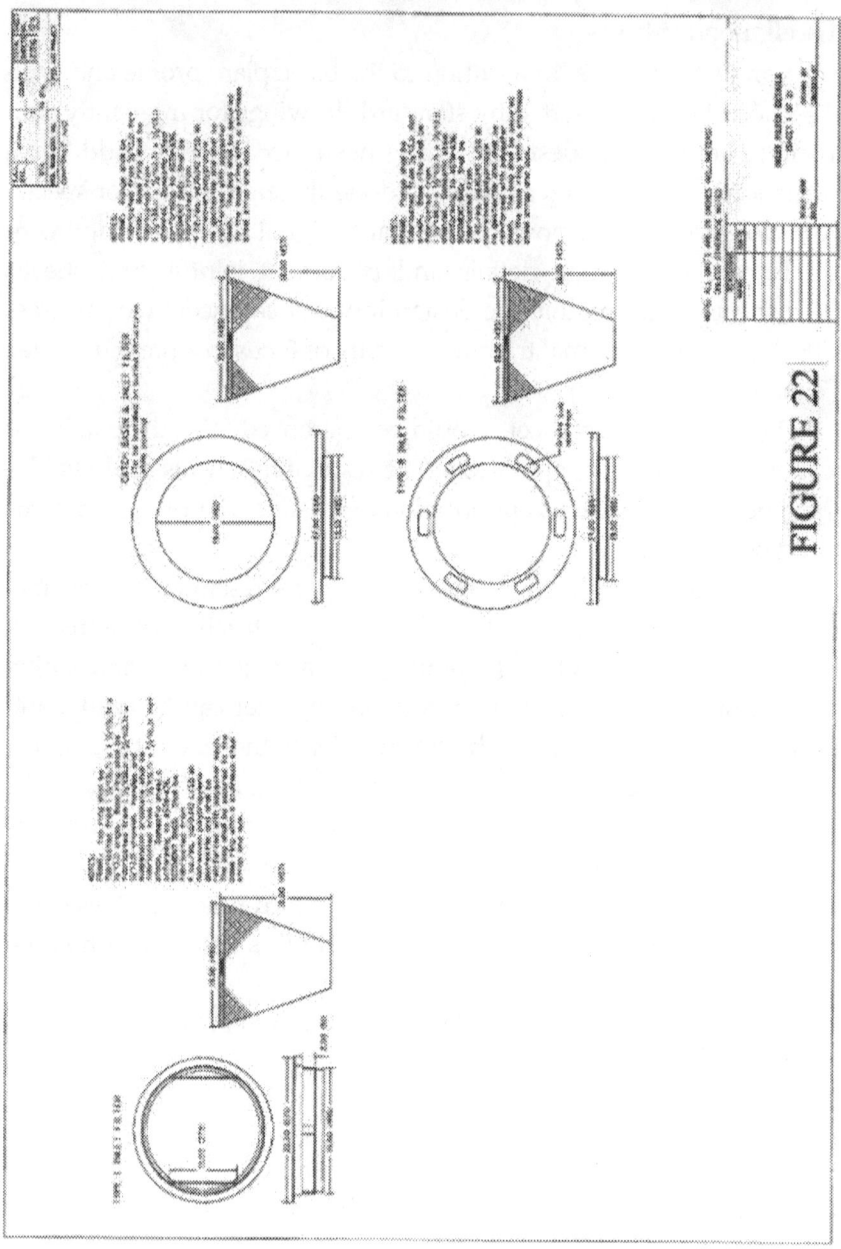

FIGURE 22

Miscellaneous Sheets

Every project is unique. In addition to the basic plan, profile and typical section sheets, supported by standard drawings for frequently constructed items, the designer may need to provide additional instructions to the contractor. This is done through the use of specialized sheets such as Removal plans, traffic signal equipment and conduit layout, intersection details and pavement joint layout sheets. These sheets might require the design input of engineers who possess skills derived from formal training or years of focus in a particular area of expertise.

The miscellaneous sheets would be referenced from the plan view location where they are applicable. The scale of the sheets could be different, but the dimensions and location of existing and proposed items would be the same.

Some agencies rely on publications that represent acceptable methods or procedures to be followed for the construction of items that have a more direct affect on the public, such as water main and sanitary sewer systems. Labor by a specialized engineer can be costly, and best minimized or focused with certainty. Once the labor is expended, it cannot be recovered if it is found that the client had a particular design guideline in mind. The client's use of publications might not be part of the agreement for services or the scope of work. It might be assumed that the engineer is familiar with standard practices. This situation might not be discovered until a submittal is made, which could result in additional labor.

A sample Miscellaneous Detail Sheet is shown in Figure 23.

Plans, Special Provisions and Contract Plan Reviews

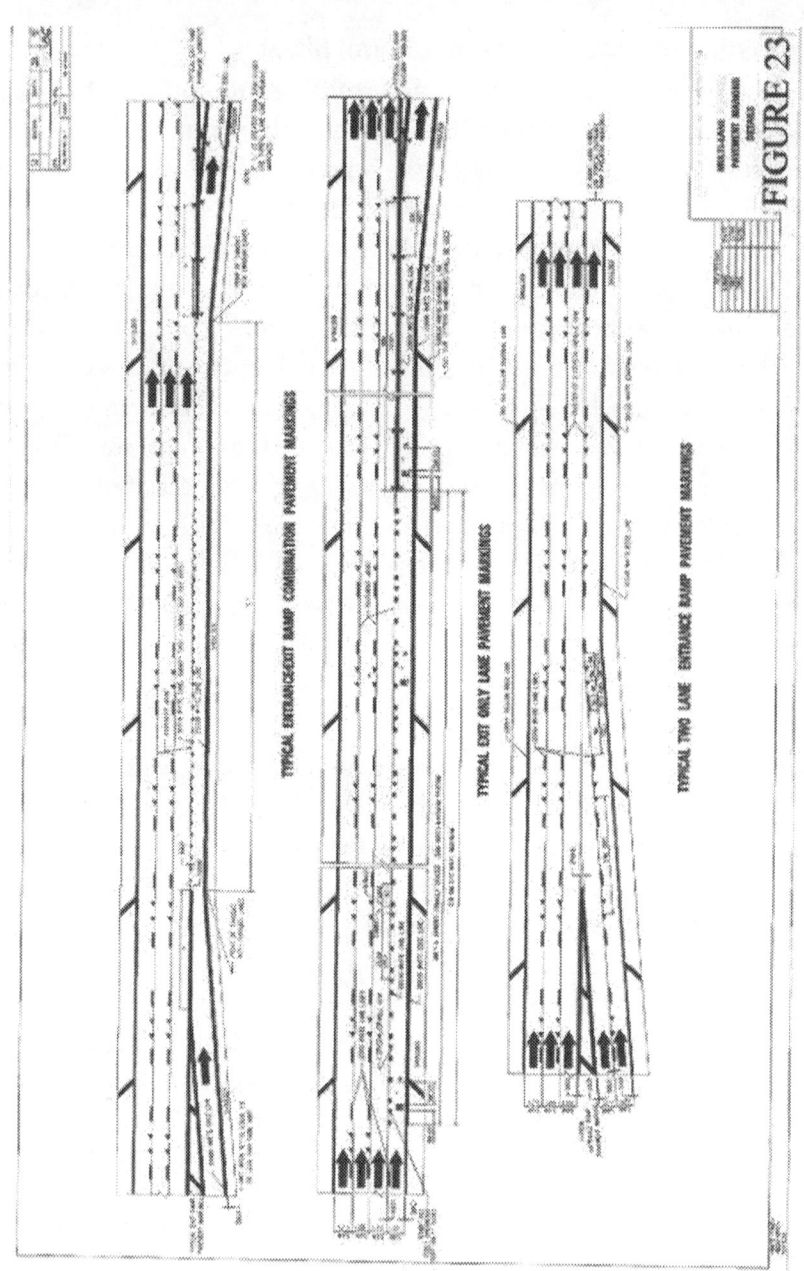

FIGURE 23

The Sediment Control / Erosion Control Sheet

Many agencies must conform to a permitting procedure that respects the conditions of the surrounding environment and provides legal assurances that a project will not have adverse effects upon the local or surrounding areas. Conformance with these procedures typically involves the use of contractual notes, specific construction operations and standardized items to be placed in accordance with approved techniques. Erosion may occur naturally, but when construction activities change the surface of a project site, the amount of erosion might increase, and must therefore be controlled until final grading and landscape activities have taken place. The need to control runoff-borne sediment might require a two-step process involving activities which are intended to prevent sediment and activities which are intended to collect accumulated sediment. Erosion would be expected to occur in any stage of construction whenever earthwork is placed or removed. Sheets may need to be developed for each stage of construction.

Sediment Control

During construction, operations such as the displacement of material, the stockpiling of topsoil, or the transfer of components from storage to the jobsite, may result in loose matter which could unintentionally become dislodged and carried away from the jobsite as storm-water runoff. In these situations, a separate set of Sediment Control Plans would be required, covering the project limits as well as any downstream locations. The Sediment Control Plans would show where the sediment would be trapped in ditches, or collected in excavated pits known as traps. The Sediment Control Plans and the accompanying notes would indicate the volume of material that would be allowed to accumulate or be trapped before removal would be required.

Plans, Special Provisions and Contract Plan Reviews

Erosion Control

In the event that grading operations will result in the placement of an embankment or a stockpile of material that will remain in place for a period of time, stabilization operations such as seeding, erosion control blankets, fabric or plastic silt fencing around the embankment or stockpile might be required. Activities such as the displacement of material, the stockpiling of topsoil, or the transfer of components from storage to the jobsite, may loosen surface matter which could unintentionally become dislodged and carried away from the jobsite as stormwater runoff. In these situations, a separate set of Erosion Control Plans, similar to the Sediment Control Plans, but representing an interim condition, would be required. In the case of temporary seeding, it is not unlikely that the newly-established vegetation would need to be removed prior to using the stockpiled materials.

A return to the field to acquire additional topographic information might be needed in the final stages of plan development, since the full impacts of sediment and erosion control might not be known until the drainage design and cross-sections have been completed.

A sample Sediment/Erosion Control Sheet is shown in Figure 24.

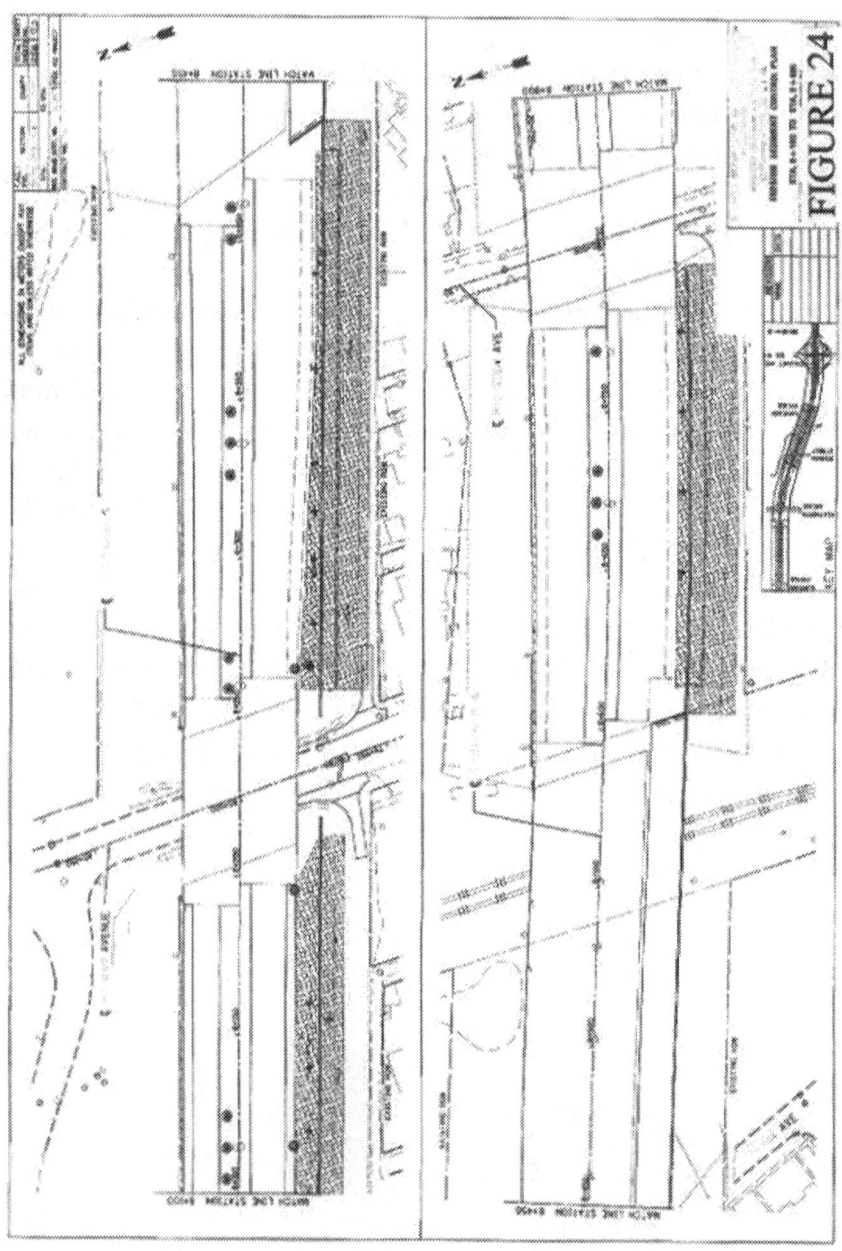

Plans, Special Provisions and Contract Plan Reviews

The Landscaping Sheet

Once a project has been constructed, it may be necessary to provide either permanent erosion control measures or vegetation enhancements that will make the project blend into its environs in a more pleasing manner. Special plantings, trees, sod and seed in parkways, particular grasses around ponds or compensatory storage areas and seeding to restore excavation sites may be placed with stations and offsets that are to be laid out as precisely as a length of curb or a paved area. Landscaping could be added to areas adjacent to paving, to embankment side-slopes, to the sides of ditches and to restore the ground at borrow or stockpile sites. The variety of planting possibilities lends itself to the use of symbols, shading and other drafting techniques such as cross-hatching or dotted patterns that might cover wide or irregularly shaped areas of the plans. If these were to be added to the Roadway Plan or the Drainage Plan or the Erosion Control Plan, vital information could become illegible. It is therefore common practice for some agencies to require that the landscape information be provided on separate sheets. Since a plan view ensures that all areas intended to be planted are covered, the Landscaping Sheet could be based on the topographic information shown on the Roadway or Drainage sheets. The stationing for layout and measurement would remain unchanged. If all of the landscape items were presented in tabular format, such as on a Schedule of Quantities sheet, the layout and measurement would still require that the landscape workers consult a plan sheet that showed the project stationing or control line in order to perform their work. The project limits for landscaping would not necessarily be the same as those shown on the paving, drainage or erosion control sheets.

Legibility becomes more of an issue when shading or textured patterns are placed over areas that are to be landscaped. The stations, offsets, widths, curve data and corners of planted areas can be provided using leaders, but the end points might be lost if the leader crosses a shaded or hatched area. Tables of data or a short-hand method of labeling could be used in an attempt to reduce the amount of text to be drafted.

Landscaping is subject to seasonal restrictions as well as watering requirements. Since the landscaping is often placed at the conclusion of other operations, the calendar might dictate that the project be landscaped the following year. This situation could have an impact on the construction completion date, the number of working days, any incentive programs for timely conclusion of construction, and can lead to unanticipated fees for layout beyond the contractual timeframes.

The incorrect selection of proper seeding and sod is also an issue which can cause labor dollars to be expended at the last minute, prior to submittal, since the landscaping could be shown in Summaries, Schedules, Erosion Control Sheets Cross-sections and Construction Staging.

A sample Landscaping Sheet is shown in Figure 25.

Plans, Special Provisions and Contract Plan Reviews

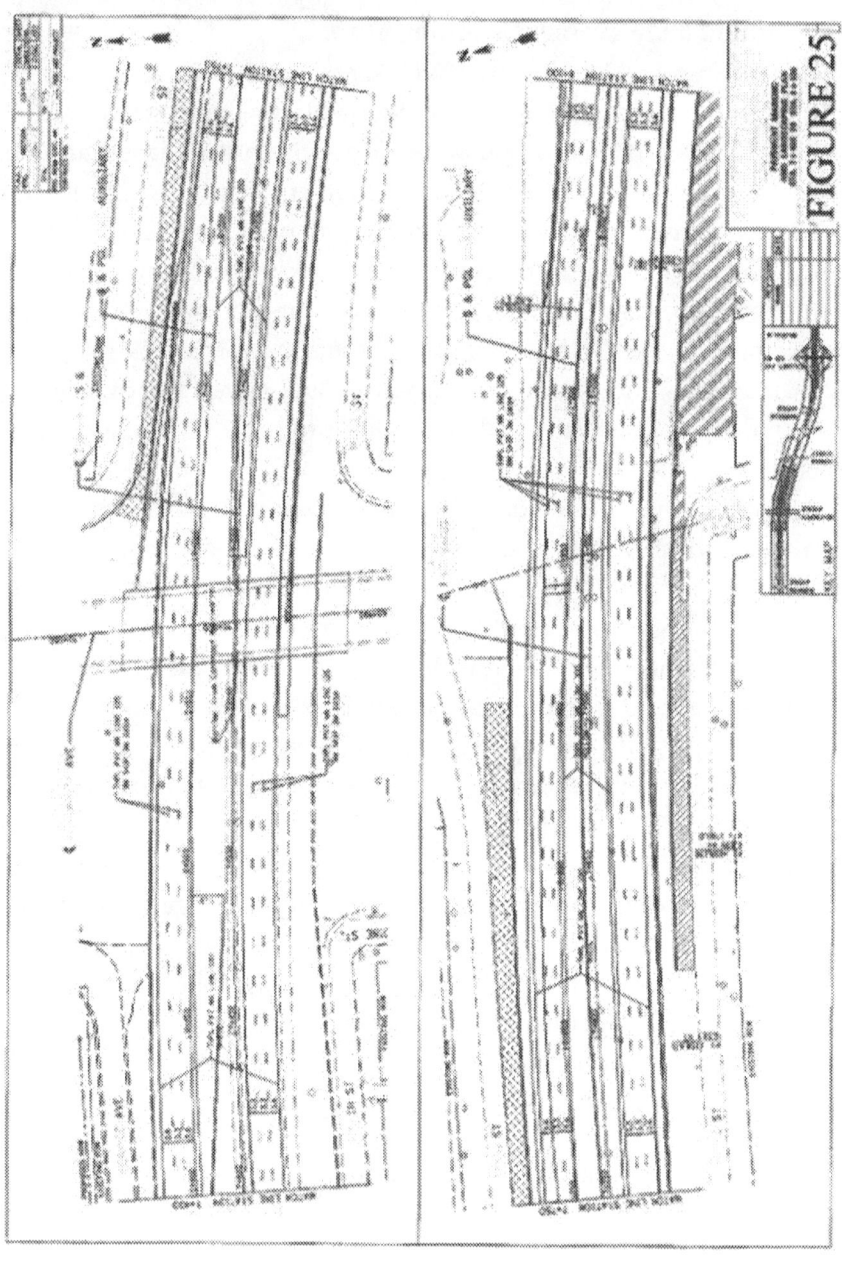

The Signing and Pavement Marking Sheet

The final finishing touches that will allow a roadway project to be opened to the motoring public include the placement of traffic control and information devices to guide vehicles within their lanes, around obstacles and on to their destinations. Pavement markings and signing is usually placed in accordance with legal precedent, and is often based on the published guidelines contained in the Manual on Uniform Traffic Devices (MUTCD). Individual states may have their own supplement to the MUTCD, showing specific preferences for pavement markings and signs. Often agencies will have their own set of preferred signs, especially if they are the producer of the sign panel stock.

Signing can be posted on light poles, on separate metal or wooden sign posts which could be driven directly into the ground, or might need to be supported by structural foundations. Signs could be attached to bridges, viaducts or overpasses, mounted on overhead trusses or attached to retaining walls along the side of the road.

Since pavement markings and signs are often complimentary, such as a stop bar on the pavement and an adjacent stop sign, it is easier to show both on the same sheet. The Signing and Pavement Marking Sheet would require stationing or other reference controls to ensure that the items were placed in the correct locations. In some instances, a plan view could present all of the visual images or symbols, while the location and layout information can be shown in tabulated form, or can be shown on the Schedule of Quantities Sheet.

Sign locations are often driven by specified dimensions suggested in guide publications such as the MUTCD. The location of the sign will need to be cross-checked with other disciplines such as drainage and lighting to avoid placement of a sign that can damage underground appurtenances, or disrupt the intended lighting coverage for a segment of roadway.

Plans, Special Provisions and Contract Plan Reviews

Sign panel dimensions will vary depending on the posted speed limit, the location of the sign and the agency's practice. A stop sign used on one project may look the same, but the size may vary. A stop sign, for instance, can be made in four different sizes, and can be special-ordered with folding capabilities for occasional use. Each size is applicable to a different situation. Certain agencies prefer one type of sign post over another, in order to minimize replacement stock. The legends or wording upon the signs would also vary depending on the size of the sign. The lettering is specifically sized to be legible from regulatory distances. Making last-minute plan revisions can affect calculations of panel sizes, method of mounting and possibly require protection such as guardrail. Knowing what the client uses can save labor dollars.

A sample Pavement Marking Sheet is shown in Figure 26.

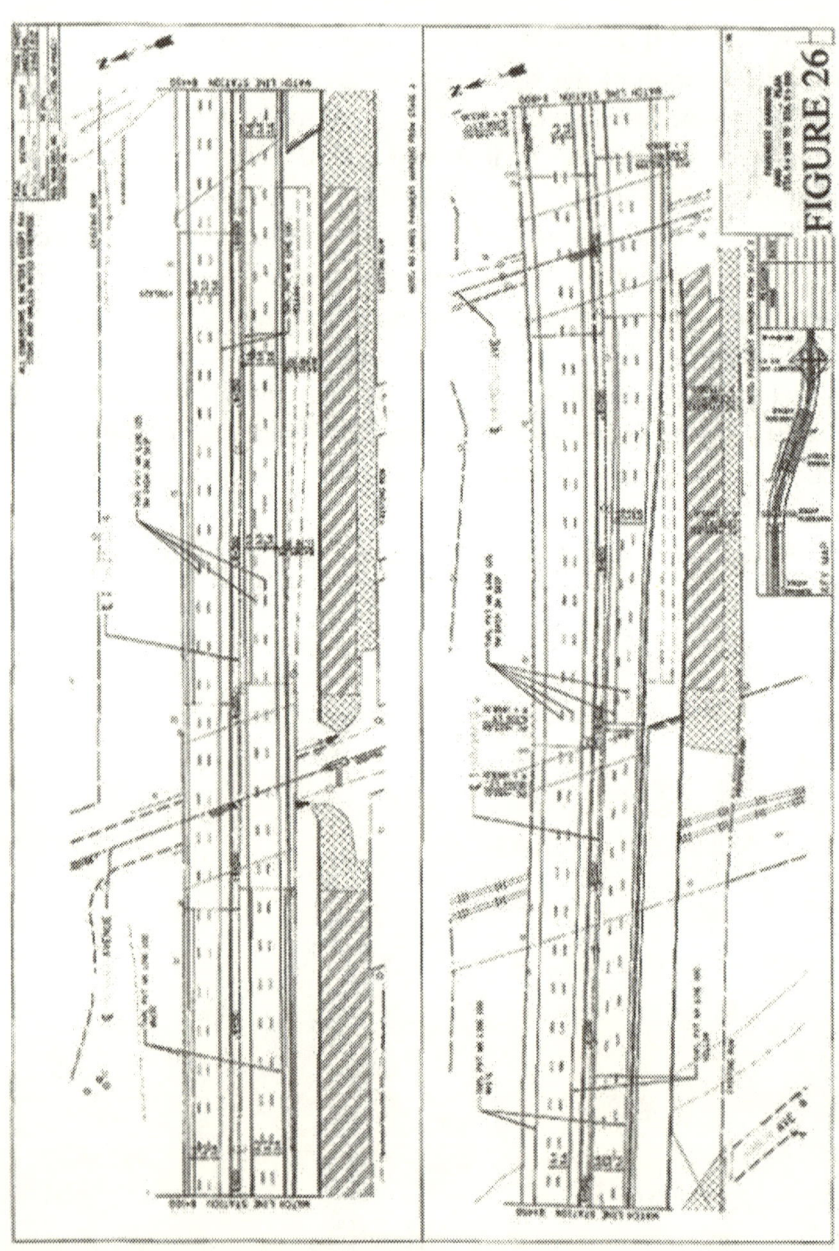

Plans, Special Provisions and Contract Plan Reviews

Right of Way Plans

Nearly all public works projects are constructed within the public right-of-way. In some cases, a permanent easement may be required in order to install an underground feature such as a sewer or water main. However, many projects require the acquisition, temporary or permanent re-grading of additional property in order to construct the proposed improvements. Drawing a line on a plan view and labeling it an "easement" does not constitute the legal procedure necessary to enter the property, construct something and walk away with the impression that the property now belongs to the public. The documents which describe the activities necessary to obtain this property have both a legal and a visual component.

The legal component might be contained within a description of the underlying property, and is often set in very exact terminology prepared by Land Surveyors in order to be able to find the boundaries of the property at some future time. Often, the legal description is quite old, perhaps going back for generations, and may refer to topography or events that were common knowledge at the time of the initial writing of the description. Wording such as "at the corner of the red barn", "under the apple tree at the edge of the second creek south of the cinder road", "beginning at the rock where Tom's horse lost a shoe", or "opposite the fence that used to be the north side of the pasture". These phrases came from actual property descriptions, and are filed in various counties in various states. The topography might well be changed, which would require that a Land Surveyor be involved in order to correctly describe the property in question.

It is therefore not enough to simply draw a line on someone's property and expect that the owner will graciously allow the contractor to enter the property to perform construction. The same premise would hold true for the removal and replacement of a private driveway from a point within the public right-of-way to the edge of the private property. A line on a drawing depicting a saw-cut at the edge of the property will not necessarily bind the contractor's workforce to stay on the public side of the property in order to perform the work. To the contrary, in some jurisdictions, setting foot on the private side of the line might be considered an act of trespass, subject to legal action, and resulting in lost time and expense to resolve the matter in a proper legal manner.

The visual component of a set of right-of-way plans resembles a set of roadway plans in that it has alignment, stationing, dimensions and relationship to existing topographic features. The stationing may be different from that used during the design, or the property corners may be set using coordinates.

Right of way might be acquired years prior to the start of design of a project, and might be referenced by coordinates or a survey station system that differs from that used in the design. A comparative check of distances and relationships to existing topography will be required in order to import the necessary information from a set of right-of-way plans into a set of construction documents. The parcel of property necessary to construct an infrastructure improvement might be a small portion of a larger tract of land. The legal description of the large tract might contain a point of beginning that is miles away from the location of the proposed improvement. This further complicates the description of an easement or a property acquisition. The stationing, property corners and ties that may appear in the legal description of property can be affected by the proposed work. In some situations, the restoration of survey monuments is the responsibility of the contractor. In other scenarios, the designer would be required to ensure that proposed work does not alter the property corners or affect the ability of the contractor to find or reset the markers at the end of the work.

Chapter Two

WRITING SPECIAL PROVISIONS

Introduction

Most clients, whether they are public agencies, public-owned utilities, private corporations or private-owned toll roads, will have a published, adopted, legal document containing the specifications by which their facilities are to be designed, constructed and maintained. These are typically called Standard Specifications, and may cover ninety percent of the work anticipated to be performed or encountered by the client during the service life of their facility. As new technology emerges, as advanced methods of construction are developed, or as materials become available to replace traditional substances, the Standard Specifications are updated, amended, appended or re-issued as a new edition. The initial phase of a revision or adaptation often takes place as a Special Provision, written for an initial use of a material or a construction technique that is being introduced. The Special Provision might be adopted as a Supplemental or Interim Standard Specification until the next edition of the Standard is published. However, many projects present the designer with a situation that does not comply with or can be defined by the current Standard Specifications, and therefore must be defined in precise terminology in order to convey the intent of the designer to the bidder and the construction team.

The following process will guide the designer in writing a Special Provision to accomplish the intended outcome.

Format

The text of a Special Provision becomes a controlling element in a legal document, binding two or more parties to the stipulations of a contractual agreement. The content of a Special Provision might be a single sentence, three or four paragraphs, or it might be several pages of inter-related and cross-referenced material. The grammar and writing structure is intended to be precise, leaving no room for misinterpretation, and may appear to be redundant in order to avoid any misdirection. Reference may be made to specific portions of the plans or to specific General Notes or additional information shown on the plans in order to avoid redundancy or in order to guide the construction team to the intended plan view so that the Special Provision is clearly understood.

The Special Provisions for a construction item describe the concepts of "What", "Where", "How to Achieve Acceptance", "With What Materials", "How to Measure the Work" and "How to Pay for the Work". The Special Provision will describe in detail or by reference: What is to be done; The Location at which the intended Work is to be performed; The procedures to be followed; The materials to be used or the allowable range of substitutions; The equipment required to produce an acceptable outcome; The method by which the extent of the completed work is to be measured; and, The basis upon which compensation for the work is to be made. A Special Provision is not intended to tell the construction team How to do the work. The bidder is expected to know the way to perform the work in order to follow the Special Provision.

The order of presentation of Construction Special Provisions may be alphabetical, or may follow the listing of pay items shown in the Summary of Quantities. In some instances, the Construction Special Provisions are grouped by type of work, by construction stage or by season, if the work is temperature or time sensitive.

Plans, Special Provisions and Contract Plan Reviews

The text may be presented in numbered paragraphs that match the numbering system of the underlying Standard Specifications. The text may be presented in bullet-point fashion or it may be numbered using a separate system that has no direct relation to the numbering system of the underlying, controlling documents. These decisions are client-specific and will vary from one project to the next.

Given the potential for using a Special Provision that has been written for similar work, it would be cost-effective for the design team to read the complete text of the Special Provision to be used, so that references to other documents are applicable and format matches the client's preferences. The fact that the title of a Special Provision in one project matches the title of a pay item in another project does not ensure that the Special Provision will define the work intended to be performed.

Types of Special Provisions
General

A general Special Provision might be written to identify the published edition of the underlying documents which are intended to control the work. It can be written to define the location of the work by county, parish, township, street and crossroad. It might be written to indicate the funding and jurisdiction for the work. It can be written to describe or list all of the types of proposed work to be performed and the coordination that might be needed with other work in the vicinity. A general Special Provision might bear an effective date indicating when it was developed or approved.

A general Special Provision can be written to identify personnel or agency departments that would need to be contacted for utility coordination, traffic signal modifications, insurance requirements, review of record plans or preliminary engineering reports, and permission to enter property such as forest preserves and parkland. It might be written to define incentives for timely completion of the work, penalties for certain conditions and financial obligations that might not be contained within the underlying control documents. It can be written to define the minimum number of lanes required to maintain traffic flow. It might be written to define procedures to be followed for accident response, snow removal and the types of repairs to existing pavement that is to remain in place and used to carry traffic.

General Special Provisions can be written to define the approval process necessary for the acceptance of an item of work, or to describe the locations to be used for stockpiling materials or obtaining electrical power. A general Special Provision might be necessary to define the need for the contractor to engage the services of a professional engineer in order to complete the design of a specific item of work, or to prepare drawings that delineate the parameters of an item to be constructed, as in the case of shop or working drawings for structural items to be fabricated.

A general Special Provision may indicate the number of calendar days, working days or provide a completion date for the project. The timeframe will need to match the suggested construction staging as well as the temperature-sensitive items in order to be enforceable.

Construction

A construction Special Provision might be written to revise a single word in the text of a Standard Specification. A construction Special Provision can be written to insert or revise a paragraph of text or to substitute a table of data. A construction Special Provision can be written to define the construction or implementation of a new item or procedure that is being introduced by an agency for the first time. A construction Special Provision might be needed to incorporate updated techniques or to modify procedures that have revised by recent developments or products that have been shown to improve the outcome.

Plans, Special Provisions and Contract Plan Reviews

Construction Special Provisions can be written for earthwork operations, paving items, drainage components, structural and electrical elements, traffic maintenance and landscaping work, as well as for the installation of appurtenances, the modification of existing facilities or the removal and relocation of an ornamental feature. In short, one may prepare a construction Special Provision to address any work to be performed that is not covered by existing text in a referenced Standard Specification publication.

For most agencies and clients, a Construction Special Provision does not define the methods by which the contractor is to perform the work. Writing such controlling terms into a Special Provision could inadvertently involve unions, legal entities, laws and ordinances which are to be complied with during the project.

Performance

A performance Special Provision might be written to advise the contractor of the minimum expectations that have been identified within a particular industry as the acceptable measure of a completed work item. A performance Special Provision can be written to insert a reference to a material or test that has recently been devised for use in the approval process for accepting a completed work item. A performance Special Provision may make direct reference to a product or manufacturer for comparison with the required work, or to alert the contractor of the proprietary nature of an element to be incorporated into the completed work.

Regulatory

A regulatory Special Provision might define the various requirements for compliance in order to achieve acceptance of public works or utility construction. These requirements could be laws, permits, ordinances or recently adopted procedures that have a controlling impact on the performance of the work. A regulatory Special Provision can identify established guidelines to be followed for public safety, for worker protection and for prevention of situations that could lead to the imposition of a fine or the loss of a permit. A regulatory Special Provision might designate ordinances that govern hours of operation, engine noise, debris removal, street cleaning, sedimentation, night work and public safety.

A regulatory Special Provision can assign responsibilities for the performance of various activities such as snow removal, mailbox restoration, material approval, permits for haul routes or oversize loads, lane closure procedures and the construction of accident investigation sites. A regulatory Special Provision can indicate penalties for non-compliance with certain stipulated activities. A regulatory Special Provision might designate the amounts and types of specific insurance coverage that would be needed to work within railroad or other agency property. A regulatory Special Provision can define the requirements for flag-persons to warn traffic or workers of on-coming traffic, delivery trucks or trains. The need for a regulatory Special Provisions is prompted by the existence of a regulation, law, permit or statute that would affect the way in which work proceeds.

A regulatory Special Provision might contain the term "as directed by the Engineer". The term "Engineer" could have multiple interpretations, such as the Resident Engineer, the design engineer who signed and sealed the plans, the client representative or the Engineer in responsible charge of all work in a particular area. In all situations, the term "Engineer' will need to be discussed with the client, in order to avoid the potential situation that could result in assigning responsibility to an unknown third party.

The Grammar of a Special Provision

A Special Provision would be written with precise syntax, avoiding vernacular, and clearly directing the reader from start to finish, so that no room is left for interpretation and all misguidance is avoided. It

Plans, Special Provisions and Contract Plan Reviews

would present the terms and conditions under which activities were to proceed. A Special Provision cannot attempt to assume that the reader knows what is in the mind of the writer by reference to similar work or recent projects. The text of the Special Provision becomes a binding article of a legal document. In most agencies, this text would be considered to take precedence over the lines, numbers and notes on a drawing. The intent of a Special Provision cannot be altered or enhanced by a public reading in which inflection or emphasis is given to a particular word or phrase.

The Special Provision can be read aloud by members of the design team to test whether the intent is clear. In the event that the reader finds the need to provide further explanation, emphasis or clarification, then it might be necessary for the text to contain such additional wording that augments the intent of the author. The construction team will not hear the emphasis that a reader places on a word or phrase in an attempt to convey additional meaning or understanding. All intent must be clearly written into the Special Provision. It is acceptable in some instances to use wording such as "…it is the intent of this Special Provision to…".

Description

The Description paragraph of a Special Provision is intended to define the extent of the intended operation. It might begin with wording such as: "This item shall consist of …". The text would proceed to describe the work to be performed, using terms such as "…in accordance with…", or "…as shown on…". The text might indicate the intended purpose of the work, as in the case of preparatory grading, clearing of a surface prior to grading, or furnishing materials to be incorporated into the work under the guidance or another Special Provision. It is not necessary to list every item or type of work to be performed. Often, a phrase such as "…all collateral and associated work necessary to complete the pay item as shown on the plans and as described herein..." will be used to indicate the need for further reading.

A sample paragraph might read "This item shall consist of the assembly of broken pieces of pottery at the locations shown on the plans, in accordance with instructions listed in the second edition of *Digging at Sites*, or as directed by the Engineer, in order to prepare a mosaic for preservation as specified herein, and shall include all incidental or collateral work necessary to complete this item to the satisfaction of the Engineer".

Location
The Location paragraph can define where work begins, ends, is omitted, matches other work or is subject to the unique field conditions that would be determined at a later date. The text might include terms such as "...at a point on the centerline...", approximately X feet from the edge of pavement...", or "...a distance of X meters from the intersection of...". The location data may refer to the plan sheets for further clarification, such as "...as shown on Sheet 5 of 45..." or "...as shown on the Typical Section...".

A sample paragraph might read "The work begins at Station 123+45.67, 89.01 feet left of the centerline of Route A, and continues south approximately 543.21 feet to the end of the culvert beneath Any Street".

Means
The standards to which the completion of work items are to conform can be described in a Special Provision without stating or defining the manner in which the work is to be done. In other words, the Special Provision can tell the contractor what to do, but normally cannot define the methods by which the work is to be accomplished. Text in the Means paragraph might contain phrases such as "...shall conform to the requirements of...", "...shall meet the various requirements of the

Plans, Special Provisions and Contract Plan Reviews

applicable articles of …", "…shall meet Section 06 or the…", or might indicate that "…the work is to be done to the satisfaction of the owner's representative…". None of this text would tell how to do the work.

The Means paragraph could also describe a mechanical component of a process, such as "The tines shall be flat and spaced three-eighths of a centimeter apart, wrapped in plastic and dragged through frozen artificial turf after use". It could describe time or temperature-sensitive procedures, as in "The agitated wash mixture shall be placed between May 23 and July17, when the ambient temperature is above 50 degrees F and rainfall has not been measurable for two hours".

A sample Means paragraph might read: "The installation shall be capable of stacking four rocks at a time and shall be checked daily, prior to the restoration of normal flow. The work shall conform to applicable Sub-Articles of the Standard Codes for Aggregate Stacks, Second Edition, and shall further meet the satisfaction of the Engineer's representative".

Materials

The materials necessary to construct a pay item are subject to inspection and approval processes, some of which are intended to be conducted by a third party, which would require that the source or the material itself would possess unique identifiable properties. In order for the completed pay item to be acceptable and to withstand any design forces for which it is designed, unique or specially-treated materials are required. Substitutions might not be permissible. Often a Materials paragraph of a Special Provision will include a direct reference to a recent publication of errata or to a supplement or interim specification, or to the existence of information which is not common knowledge. Such a situation could be generated by the actions of a single individual who might have attended a training session where a new approved material or procedure was unveiled. Disseminating the information throughout the design and construction industry could take time. It would be incumbent upon the writer of the Special Provision to share the knowledge within the organization, or with the client, in order to avoid having the text rejected by an uninformed reader.

The text of a Materials paragraph may contain phrases such as: "...shall meet the requirements of Sub-Article ABC, Table 1...", or "...meeting the approval of the Engineer...", or "Article 5 of the Recurring Standards shall be modified to read...". The way in which the material is received or stored on site may be specified with phrases such as: "...shall deliver to the site on the dates indicated...", "...shall be stored in an enclosed...', "...handled in accordance with the precautions stipulated in...", or "...shall be responsible for the protection of the material from the elements...". Design criteria could be cited as in: "...and shall be capable of bearing 4 kips per unit area...".

A sample Materials paragraph might read: "The bracing shall be fabricated as detailed on Sheet 7 and shall be delivered during off-peak hours. Lifting of the units shall conform to the codes of Local Union 3. Storage shall meet the applicable Articles of the Compliance Codes. The length of each brace member shall not exceed a dimension that is twice the height of the shortest exposed surface of the Improvement".

Measurement

The area surrounding a particular item of work, such as the trench for the installation of a sewer, or a spillway to be covered in dumped riprap, might not conform to the exact lines and detailed dimensions shown on the plans. In order to avoid any misconception or misunderstanding during construction, the plans may identify the limits of payment for which compensation will be made. Some agencies will have tabular quantities or guidelines for similar work that is common to an area, or is of a repetitious nature and cannot be misinterpreted. Having dimensions specified might limit the use of certain methods of operations, such as using a large trenching implement instead of a

Plans, Special Provisions and Contract Plan Reviews

smaller one. As in all typical Special Provisions, the methods to be used to achieve approval are not indicated. For example, the plans would suggest that a nine-foot wide trench be excavated, but would not tell that a three-foot or a twelve-foot wide device would be used. The plans would, however, indicate that payment for the work would be limited to the nine-foot width. Information of this type becomes critical for a bidder scheduling the use of equipment, and affects the cost of doing the work.

A Measurement paragraph might indicate that work "...shall be measured in cubits in accordance with...", or "...shall be measured for payment along a line parallel to and 3 inches beyond...", or "...shall be measured at 30-foot increments along the ...". Storage periods, lane closures or delivery timeframes can also be measured for payment.

A sample Measurement paragraph could read: "This item of work shall be measured for payment in square meters, not to exceed a boundary of four meters parallel to the paved edge. Broken corners shall be measured and the area deducted from the area for which payment will be made".

Basis of Payment

There is a multitude of units by which a work item can be paid, including the measure of actual hours and documented costs involved. For most projects that are to be constructed under a bid situation, the means of payment will directly affect the work methods incorporated by the contractor. Items that are time-sensitive might require higher level of skill and more experienced input than items which are measured on a completion basis and are constructed with basic skills. Placing dumped rip-rap and placing trench backfill represent different skill sets and expertise. The basis of payment could be the volume of material placed, but the measured parameters would be defined in different ways.

A Basis of Payment paragraph might indicate that other work not mentioned, but understood to be required, will be included within the unit of measurement, as in the case of a concrete sidewalk placed on a prepared gravel bed and scored with transverse joint lines at five-foot intervals.

A sample Basis of Payment paragraph might read: "This work will be paid for at the contract unit price per acre for GREEN GRASS, which price shall be considered as payment in full for all labor, equipment and materials necessary to complete the work as specified herein. No additional compensation shall be made for removing grass seed from the tops of drainage frames and lids, or for the replacement of grass seed that leaves the area on the tires of watering equipment". The title of the pay item is often shown in capital letters, bold font or italics, and will match the name of the pay item in the Summary of Quantities so that there is no misunderstanding regarding the work or payment.

Some clients might request that a Special Provision be provided for each pay item. The Special Provision may be one sentence that indicates the applicable Standard Specification that controls the work. The design teams will have read the Standard Specifications as they develop their particular pay items. Unless the client has asked for this type of presentation, it is an expenditure of labor dollars that can be avoided by asking for clarification.

The intended outcome can be clear in the mind of the designer, or it can be seen by the designer at a nearby site. The challenge facing the designer is to verbally describe the intended outcome, since the designer can not converse with the bidder, or take the bidder to see what the designer has in mind. The grammar cannot use terms that are subject to knowledge that the bidder may not possess.

Use of terms such as "incidental', "as directed by the Engineer", "as specified herein" and "to the satisfaction of the Engineer" are limited to situations where such wording is acceptable to the client. Cer-

Plans, Special Provisions and Contract Plan Reviews

tain agencies have discontinued the use of the term "incidental". Others have discontinued any reference to "direction by the Engineer". Some have excluded any reference to an Engineer on the site and recognize that the "satisfaction" of one individual may not be the same as that measured by another individual, since this terminology is subject to interpretation and might affect the manner in which a bid was prepared or submitted.

Chapter Three

PERFORMING CONTRACT PLAN REVIEWS

Introduction

No two sets of plans for similar projects are exactly alike. They may both be prepared for a similar type of roadway project and may differ by a street name, the stationing interval or a single digit in a funding code, but they will not be exactly alike. Using one set as a guide for the review of the other set may not always provide suitable results.

The staff of two design teams or two construction teams working on similar projects might not be the same. They may have the same project manager or superintendent, but it is possible for one of the team members to be re-assigned from another project, and for that member to have more or less experience than the other team members.

No single checklist of items will cover all types of sets of infrastructure or roadway plans. Some checklist phrase or suggested review comment can trigger an awareness of another item that might need to be checked, while other comments might generate revisions on sheets that have not been submitted for review, or change the selection of a construction detail or the title of a pay item. A firm or agency may have a published Quality Guidelines Manual which might indicate that reviews will be performed, could include checklists for verification and might require that reviewers of drawings will use color codes to ensure that items have been checked, corrected or approved. In

Plans, Special Provisions and Contract Plan Reviews

most instances, the actual process for checking, and the potential anomalies that might occur, are generally not part of the publication.

Each line on each sheet must be followed from edge-to-edge of the sheet, as well as checking at the match lines of each sheet to ensure that the line did not change or get overlooked. The line symbol and label cannot change from sheet to sheet. Using stationing at the match lines for each sheet rather than using sheet numbers will alleviate last minute corrections. The relative size or volume of the item represented by each line needs to be understood, since a two-inch gas service line might look the same as a sixty-inch force main. The two items would not occupy the same space. Conflicts and contradictions can be seen if line work is compiled in the logical order of construction operations. Line symbols added to sheets in the latter stages of development often change from sheet to sheet, or are not labeled the same from one sheet to the next, leading to an apparent contradiction and potential loss of communication to the contractor.

Reviews can be performed by upper management, construction staff or by a team of peers with similar experience. The design team might have anticipated that construction will be sequenced in a particular order, but if that order is not made mandatory by a Special Provision, the contractor may submit a different sequence or staging, the staging might be approved, and a change order may be needed in order to accommodate the approved staging.

Personal pride and ego will contribute more to contradictions and anomalies in a set of contract documents than anything else. No one wants to have their work shown to be deficient, or have their work questioned. The tendency in some organizations will cause a team to withhold their portion of work until the last minute, hoping that it can get submitted too late for any revisions, or without having to defend their work. This action prevents an objective review of the completed work, and might lead to contradictions within a set of plans. Anyone can agree that "errors" are possible in the practice of any discipline of engineering. The key is for those "errors" to be found prior to submittal, and for the firm to refrain from criticism of the "error', and to view the finding as a positive action which avoided a potential costly situation.

Even the most objective, best-intentioned review can result in a confrontational situation, most likely caused by a bruised ego or a protective over-reaction to the discovery of a flaw. There are various ways to prevent confrontations, such as: with-holding opinions, commentaries, anecdotes and comparisons; avoiding the urge to justify a review comment or re-design an anomaly; and, ensuring that the observed anomaly is in fact displayed on the final product and does not represent work in progress. A simple circling of an element on a sheet does not convey a message, unless that message relates to a misspelling or contradiction on the dame sheet. The use of encouragement rather than criticism will aid the process and may lead to more opportunity for the plan reviewer to render further assistance in the preparation and review of other plan documents. Avoidance of the use of editorial comments in the review, or the use of words such as "never", "should" and "don't" will also help foster an educational experience rather than a critical one. The reviewer will be in the position to apply knowledge based on experience, and must not be placed in a position of defending comments that are made on the obvious anomaly.

Field Check
The most direct method that can be used to review a set of contract drawings is to conduct a plan-in-hand field check, verifying every line and symbol that is shown on the sheet, and look at the project limits to see what is being matched at the project limits. A second method would involve reviewing a photo-log or video of the project site, but the coverage of the photography may not be as thorough as needed to ensure seeing all items.

Plans, Special Provisions and Contract Plan Reviews

If time and budget permitted, the entire design team, or at least the project engineers representing each discipline, and at the very minimum, the project manager, could read the scope of work, and then walk the project from end-to-end prior to beginning design activities. Each person sees the project from the perspective of their design specialty, and would generate ideas, questions or make educated decisions based on the knowledge derived from the field. Pavement designers would note the type of paved surfaces, driveways, parking lots and roadside appurtenances. Drainage designers would note the indications of an enclosed drainage system, standing water or overland flow routes. Landscape designers would see the types of trees or the condition of existing plantings in order to assess the ability of the project site to sustain growth of proposed materials. This single event can avoid many of the review comments that are received from the client, and can preserve labor dollars in the budget.

Team Meetings

An understanding of the intended scope of work is crucial to communicate the nature of the project to each member of the design team. Changes in scope might take place during initial or subsequent negotiations or meetings that could have an effect on the work produced. The design criteria to be followed, the client's preferences for sheet content, scale and format, and local construction expectations for layout and "incidental work" are all issues that will need to be discussed so that all work can be assembled into one set of documents. Some team members might be more familiar with county projects, others with state projects and still others with federal-funded urban projects. All of the various types of funding programs might have particular preferences for sheet content, symbols and level of redundancy. A team meeting would be the appropriate time to raise questions about conflicting items that appear on the screen or might be shown on a data level that is not used by more than one discipline.

Each design task corresponds with a budget line item. The budget usually provides the labor required to perform the design task one time. A contingency might be included in the budget for overall revisions, but each design task would not have a contingency. Assignment and follow-up of each design task will ensure that last minute revisions are avoided. Adding the term "by the Engineer" simply postpones the decision to a later date, and can result in a change order.

Sheet Reviews

When drawings were drafted by hand, each original sheet could be overlaid on another sheet to compare line-work using a light table or a window. This technique might not be feasible with reduced-scale plots that are generated by design software. At this time, computer-aided design and drafting software does not have the ability to verify accuracy. Each sheet will need to be reviewed by eye, and the contents compared with other sheets that show the same view. If the layer that shows a conflicting item is turned off during design activities, and then the layer is not turned on, the conflict may go un-noticed and not be discovered or resolved.

Drawing review often leads to confrontation. No one wants their work questioned. No one wants their level of expertise exposed. The reviewer can only remark on what is seen, not on what was intended to be shown. Experience can be tapped from within the organization, or it can be gained from the project.

Each sheet in a set of plans will need to be reviewed as a stand-alone item, as well as an integral part of a complete set of contract documents. Cross-referencing to other sheets in the same set, or references to other drawings in other sets of plans needs to be precise.

Anomalies

Checklists may vary from firm to firm, or from agency to agency. No single list can be expected to cover all of the possible anomalies, con-

Plans, Special Provisions and Contract Plan Reviews

traditions or conflicting information that can appear in a set of contract documents. The following text illustrates examples of situations that were encountered, often repeatedly, during the reviews of hundreds of sets of preliminary engineering reports and contract plans over a span of nearly three decades. Rather than suggest that each element of a sheet be "checked", "verified" or "reviewed", each sheet is provided with a list of prompts to assist the reviewer in resolving anomalies that have been observed on various project. The reviewer can assemble a checklist or use the following list of prompts as a guide for applicable situations. The caution required involves checking an item thoroughly versus checking that an item exists.

Questions for Reviewers

During the course of reviewing hundreds of sets of contract plans, the number and type of questions that arise continues to grow. As mentioned above, the content of a checklist varies, and cannot be all-encompassing. No singular class or seminar can produce a complete list of situations that can arise on the various sheets of a set of plans. Questions from the staff, the client and from internal reviewers can help to produce a set of contract documents that contains fewer contradictions, anomalies or conflicts, and the questions can also be used as a training aid.

Questions that have arisen in real design situations include:

Who should sign and seal the plans? In most licensing jurisdictions, the person who seals the plans is the person under whose direction the plans were prepared. In some smaller firms, the decision on sealing plans is based on the insurance coverage carried by the firm. A person would be best-served by reading the engineering licensing law that governs their particular jurisdiction. In some situations, the application of a seal remains valid for many years, and can be affected by changes in a firm's ownership. If a person seals a set of plans and leaves the organization, the seal and any professional liabilities attached might remain that person's responsibility.

Why is a professional seal needed on a set of plans? A set of plans for an infrastructure project is designed to serve the public good. The licensing act or law establishing the jurisdiction for the practice of engineering will be very clear on this issue, as well as on many other issues pertaining to the application of a seal.

Why can't the client always sign the plans? In some jurisdictions, professional liability insurance is calculated based on the number of sets of plans or the total construction value – the amount of potential liability – that a person might have. It would therefore be in a client's best interest to limit their exposure, in the event that they decided to enter private practice and begin sealing their own plans.

What difference does it make if the client's title is not exact? For some agencies or jurisdictions, the issue of professional liability takes precedence. There may be a clause in the enabling legislature that mentions a specific stake-holder as the identified party to whom all issues of liability will defer. Identifying a person other than the one intended could result in legal complications that could be costly and time-consuming to resolve.

What difference does it make if the designation of the project does not match the designation in other documents? Some agencies are very particular when matters of project designations are concerned. For instance, a single digit in a project code might direct all documentation regarding the project to a particular archive, and the loss of documentation as a result of a misfiling could be costly.

Where does one find the official title of the project? Some project titles change from the design phase to the construction phase, so it is necessary to read the agreement for services in order to identify the exact project title used by the client.

Who assigns the project number? Typically, the client or agency awarding the project will assign a project number. The engineering

Plans, Special Provisions and Contract Plan Reviews

firm might have a completely different identification or job number for the project.

Why should the title of the sheet match the title shown in the Index? In some situations,

Will the next person hired on the project know more about the client's requirements?

Is it necessary to be exact when referencing external specifications?

If work is done in other areas of the world, why might there be a concern for the use of the client's pay item terminology?

Where is the flow-line in a rip-rap-lined ditch?

Can the edge of a gravel road be used as a tie point?

Won't the contractor be able to infer what was intended by the plans?

Do italics convey the inflection that is meant to emphasize a point in the text of a General Note or Special Provision?

The following phrases are intended to offer suggestions for issues to be reviewed, for checklists to include, or for a guide in the review of various plan sheets. Each phrase could be supported by a lengthy discussion of the situations that lead to the comment. It is left to the reader to use the phrases as prompts for thought or discussion during the review process. The intent is to share situations common to many projects that have been reviewed over the years. In all cases, the overriding guideline remains: THE CLIENT KNOWS BEST.

Title Sheet

The Title of the Project is specific, it matches the title shown in official documents such as the Agreement, Scope and Special Provisions

The Funding agency, State or local governing body is listed in proper terms and is not identified as a department when it is a division, or is listed with the proper titular head such as a commissioner or a district engineer.

The requirements for the Design Designation are addressed and match all calculations submitted as supporting documentation for the design of the project.

The Design and Posted Speed are listed for coordination with lane width and sign sizes, and match the existing ordinances that may pertain to the roadway under consideration.

The Traffic Data matches the preliminary information or is updated by recent traffic counts to substantiate the design data.

The Project Limits are consistent with the work shown on the plan drawings and matches the text that describes the scope of work.

Street names match the topography used on each drawing. Avenues, Lanes, Courts, Circles and Boulevards have legal definition in some jurisdictions, and can mislead or misrepresent the focus of a project.

Current mapping is provided, showing major route numbers and approach roadways in sufficient detail to find the project on a map.

The gross and net lengths of roads or infrastructure that is affected by the project and is consistent with the project scope of work.

Determine who will sign and seal the plans and which parties are representing the individual disciplines, the design team and the client.

The total number of sheets that is included in the complete set of contract documents may need to account for client-inserted sheets such as Standard Drawings, or Sheets that are labeled as "A" and "B" sheets.

Index of Sheets

Each Title of each drawing that is listed matches each title shown on the individual sheet title block in order to avoid misdirection.

Titles of referenced material or acceptable industry guidelines are current and applicable to the project.

Plans, Special Provisions and Contract Plan Reviews

The number of sheets listed matches the total number of sheets included in plan, including any sheets added by an addendum.

Sheets such as ROW plans and Soil Borings might need to be included if they are referenced in the description of the project.

Sheets listed as "NOT USED" might not constitute a sheet to be counted in the total in some situations, dependent on the agency or client.

The sheets listed address the entire scope of work, and include sheets representing the work of all of the disciplines from which input is needed.

Sheets to be included by others, such as those sheets prepared by sub-consultants or by the client, might need to be included in the total number of sheets that is listed in the Index.

The references on each sheet to details and standards are addressed as needed in quantities, cost allocations or work that is intended to be included in the overall cost of the project.

A listing of Standard Drawings, reference drawings, Soil Boring Logs, Utility Atlases, As-constructed file drawings and preliminary study exhibits which might affect the work may need to be included in the Index.

General Notes

References to manuals, standards and memoranda will need to be current and can not contradict or counter-direct the intended activities or outcome of the project.

The need for redundancy varies with each client, and will have to be checked in the final edition of the contract documents to ensure that each reference does not present a contradiction.

Contradictions can be contained in redundancies, so each note and reference must be checked to ensure that the total project is defined.

Clients have preferences for inclusion of preliminary commitments from public meetings, such as screening fences, hours of operation, access to the project, notification of property owners and replacement options.

Notes may apply to both design and construction activities, and are often originated as commitments that are made during the approval stages of the project.

A useful quality check is to have someone read the notes backwords to check for spelling errors.

Read the notes out loud, or have someone read the notes out loud, without inflection, to ensure that the intended message is clear.

Dramatic pauses and inflection cannot convey the design intent to the reader of the plan note or special provision during construction operations.

Summary of Quantities

The Pay Item titles need to exactly match the client standards, specifications and special provisions to avoid a claim for extra work.

The Pay Item numbers need to exactly match the Pay Item based on the specified method of measurement, e.g., tons, square yards, etc.

Rounding that is used in Pay Item quantities will need to correspond with the client criteria or allowances for overages, yield and compaction.

The drawings and Special Provisions will need to be checked to ensure that any Pay Items that are contained in referenced Standard Drawings and standardized industry details are included in the quantities, in order to avoid change orders to complete the work.

The exact listing of Pay Items and quantities needs to be obtained from each design discipline to compile the final quantities.

Construction Codes need to match the intended funding participation, such as federal, state, local or grant sources.

Plans, Special Provisions and Contract Plan Reviews

Pay items referenced in the Special Provisions and boiler plate checklists need to be included in the final quantities.

The percentage of funding participation and local matching may need to be verified to avoid exceeding appropriated budgets.

Pay Item timeframes for seasonal or temperature-related performance will need to match the project duration in months, calendar or working days. For instance, concrete curing time might exceed contract durations or might be impacted by temperatures at the end of a construction season.

There may be duplications of Pay Item titles for some work items that are used in specific operations, such as protective coatings used for structural steel or for finished concrete surfaces.

The preparation of Alternate bid packages may require the inclusion of separate Quantity Sheets.

Schedules of Quantities

The rounding applied to Pay items shown on a Schedule of Quantities will need to match the rounding shown on the Summary of Quantities in order to avoid change orders or extra work orders.

It may be necessary to group similar work items together in order to ensure that work performed by specialty contractors is scheduled at the same time.

Inverts, offsets and stations will need to match the information provided on the plan views for each structure or appurtenance.

Reflect the individual quantity calculations, traffic staging and directions of traffic flow in the Schedules of Quantities, since these may affect the overall quantity of work to be performed.

Use the totals for each Pay Item listed in the Schedules as a lead-in to the quantity that is shown on the Summary of Quantities.

The construction and removal of temporary items may need to be tabulated and summarized for payment.

The units of measure will need to be correlated with the calculations, the Schedules and the Summary of Quantities.

Discrepancies can be found when it is understood that a designer calculates a Pay Item as a line item, sheet by sheet or stage by stage, and enters the total in the Summary or Schedule of Quantities. By contrast, the Contractor preparing a bid might review each of the quantities by line item and then perform a search for the location of each item in the plans.

The Designer typically prepares the total quantity based on the addition of all calculations. Whereas, the contractor might prepare a bid price based on the location of work as shown in the plans.

Typical Sections

Compare each proposed Typical Section to the preliminary typical sections shown in the planning stage or design report to ensure that the designed work matches the intended project.

The direction of the view of a Typical Section can be "mirror-image" or can be shown looking down-station or can be shown looking North. Views may be directed by the client to face down-station, north or south.

The Typical Section will need to be coordinated with the pavement composition that is shown in Standard Drawings or Special Provisions.

Each Typical Section needs to be compared to the cross sections to determine where the section is actually "typical", and where supplemental sections may need to be provided.

The traffic data will need to correspond with the proposed pavement type to ensure that the proposed pavement provides the intended service.

Legends and symbols may vary between existing and proposed views of the same location.

Plans, Special Provisions and Contract Plan Reviews

The designer will need to identify the location of controlling criteria such as centers of construction or the Profile Grade Line relative to property centerline, survey line or other control lines.

The range of a variable width item needs to be defined in all views.

Clear zones need to be coordinated with roadside barriers.

The leader arrows and line-work needs to be followed from the corresponding notes to the intended work item. Similar checking is needed for components identified by letters or numbers.

The location of proposed sidewalk may need to be re-aligned around trees that are intended to remain in place. The re-alignment could place the sidewalk on private property or could encroach closer to a street.

The ROW width needs to match the width shown on the plan views, the cross sections and the ROW plats.

To avoid misrepresentation, it is desirable to show the layers of proposed pavement composition in relative thicknesses.

Layout and Alignment

Ensure that the proposed alignment fits within the existing (or proposed) ROW.

The bearings of property lines between ROW corners need to be verified if they are shown on a sheet having a north arrow.

The ROW Plats need to match the project cross-sections.

The back of curb and the face of curb are two distinct locations.

The top of rail is not the same as the top of track tie or top of ballast.

The location of a control point can be misinterpreted if it is not exactly described, e.g. top of flange bolt or top of hydrant.

Every attempt needs to be made to avoid the placement of control points in traffic lanes or inaccessible locations.

A street with proposed work that is controlled by stationing needs to have alignment and ties in order to properly locate the work.

Proposed detention ponds may need control points or alignment and ties in order to be constructed.

The elevation of the top of a fire hydrant may change if the fire hydrant is opened after the elevation is established by survey.

Survey ties often contain more detailed information than topographic survey data, and can often show discrepancies with the plan view.

The designer needs to define the location of stationing, e.g., baseline, survey line, construction line, center of ROW, center of roadway, etc.

Benchmarks

The topography that is shown for a survey benchmark might not match the topography that is shown in the Plan View.

A post-design Field Check might not verify the presence of a benchmark if a lengthy amount of time has elapsed between survey and final design.

Proposed construction operations might eliminate a benchmark on the first day of project implementation, or a project materials staging area might obliterate a benchmark.

Clearing and tree removal operations may obliterate a benchmark.

Traffic Control

The work zone needs to cover the intended construction shown on the proposed Typical Sections.

The locations of traffic control devices that are to be placed beyond the project limits will need to be field-checked to ensure that the intended measures are achieved.

Plans, Special Provisions and Contract Plan Reviews

The Work Area needs to be sufficient to allow for clearance to be provided for a flagger between a work zone and traffic lanes.

The Work Area needs to be sufficient to allow for moving barricades and barrier wall without encroachment into traffic lanes.

Support surfaces need to be sufficient for the placement of barrier wall, impact attenuators, barricades, traffic cones and barrels.

Barricades cannot be placed on embankment slopes that are too steep to support them.

Driveway entrances that are hidden by barricades may need supplemental signing to allow ingress and egress.

Permissible left turn movements may be prevented by lane reductions that are included in traffic staging.

Traffic staging needs to be reviewed to avoid the placement of proposed pavement markings under traffic conditions.

Covering existing or contradicting signs that are not needed is often overlooked and can result in confusion in the construction area.

Traffic staging needs to be reviewed to determine if sign panels on existing overhead trusses are located over appropriate traffic lanes.

Accident investigation sites or recovery-re-action sites may be needed to allow for areas to handle vehicle problems.

Advance public notification or warning may be needed prior to changing traffic staging overnight.

Required turn lanes might not be provided on detour routes.

Detour route signing needs to convey traffic around the project in both directions of travel.

Truck restrictions need to be checked on detour routes.

Traffic signal modifications might be needed for detours.

Construction staging needs to account for all of the work that is shown or described on all sheets, notes or Special Provisions.

Lane configurations, widths and barricades need to continue through the match lines from one sheet to the next.

Taper rates can not be altered to fit the available topography without potentially violating criteria.

The placement of traffic cones or barricades across structures may be restricted by the shoulder width on the structure.

Traffic surveillance may be needed to restore signing or re-align barricades during the absence of construction operations.

Pedestrian traffic and access to local residences needs to be addressed.

Parking for businesses and local residences needs to be addressed.

Traffic Protection for specialty work, landscaping and punch list items needs to be included in the project.

Locations of entry points for material delivery may need to be designated and verified by a field check.

Flagging operations cannot be conducted from exposed positions.

Flagger personnel are often forced to move into traffic lanes by proposed paving operations.

Parking of personal vehicles in the work zone needs to be addressed.

A clear line of sight between flaggers is needed on two-lane projects.

Paving Plans

Follow each leader line and read each callout for each note.

Compare the work description or callout to the Pay Item.

Allow for the extension of sub-base to collect sub-surface drainage.

Provide a station and offset for each change in proposed width, direction or type of paved item.

Compare the Pay Item to the Special Provision and the detail.

Construction Stationing is to be the same in each view.

Saw cuts may need to be provided at the project limits.

Plans, Special Provisions and Contract Plan Reviews

The depth of scoring for surface removal may result in an excess of pavement to be removed.

Butt joints are not always required on pavement that is to be broken and seated.

Patching is normally not performed on lanes that are to be removed.

Proposed paved widths need to match existing paved widths or have tapers at the ends of the project.

Compacted thickness of bituminous pavement can be compared with the calculated tonnage to ensure that adequate quantity is provided.

The proposed pavement type needs to match the existing pavement at the project limits in order for the correct jointing to be selected.

Access for the various paving machines, delivery of material and cleanup of tracked debris needs to be considered.

Construction vehicle weight may damage the adjacent pavement that is intended to remain in place.

Paving in areas surrounded by active traffic lanes requires substaging to allow construction access.

Vehicles wash-out areas that are beyond proposed erosion control measures need to be addressed to avoid permit violations.

Profiles

Setting changes in paving grades that exceed the capability of normal paving equipment.

The profile grade line needs to be maintained in all paving views, including the view that is shown on the cross sections.

A constant profile is not typical while crossing intersecting streets.

The profile at the project limits needs to match the profile of the existing street in order to avoid standing water conditions.

Profiles of intersecting ramps need to account for super-elevation.

Driveway grades that vary from the intersecting street can present conditions that will scrape the underside of vehicles.

The profile must match structural elements such as joints, approach pavements and shoulders at bridge abutments.

Paving operations rely on identifying super-elevation transitions by providing the beginning and ending stations.

Labeling the length of a vertical curve on the profile will serve as a check of paving limits.

Coordination with horizontal geometry is essential for paving.

The paving grades at railroad crossings need to account for both the track height and the top of rail tie.

The bottoms of piers and footings can be exposed by ditch grading.

Drainage

Storm sewer construction proceeds from low to high inverts.

Sewer diameter cannot exceed typical manholes diameter.

Introducing siphons to enter existing openings in structures usually violates hydraulic gradients.

It is customary to differentiate between sewer, pipe and culvert.

Adjusting frames or reconstructing risers may be required.

Rotating structure cones may be needed to align with gutter flow.

Structure lids need to match pavement cross-slope.

Cone sections under paved areas present compaction problems.

Frames in gutters need to match curb types.

Compaction around cone sections is necessary in embankments.

Construction or personal vehicle traffic across trench backfill areas can result in deflection of the sewer, pipe or culvert.

Cutting sewers to two-decimal lengths is usually ignored in the field.

Specify whether the elevation of a structure is set at the edge of pavement, face of curb or gutter line.

Plans, Special Provisions and Contract Plan Reviews

Grades of ditches beyond construction limits need to match incoming or out-letting flow-lines.

Placement of trench backfill within proposed embankment alters compaction of material.

The width of a trench is based on the method of sewer installation.

Trenching in front of retaining walls will alter soil conditions.

Unintended tree removal may be caused by trenching operations.

Inverts differ at the bottom of a pipe bell or spigot.

Avoid under drain connections to enclosed systems that are intended to be removed.

Incoming flow is not easily collected by flared end sections.

The water surface in a rip-rap area is not at the top of stone.

Avoid blind or wye connections to dissimilar sewer types.

Turns, bends and radii for sewer are sometimes specified beyond the recommended limits for the class or type of sewer.

There is often a recommended jointing material at utility crossings.

Steel casings are typically placed beneath railroad ballast.

Leakage can be anticipated in curved layout of sewers.

Water-main quality sewer might include ductile iron or poly vinyl pipe, which in turn might require specific materials or testing.

The specified class and type of pipe matches plans and intended use.

Center of structure or center of frame and lid are different locations.

A Station point is required on large appurtenances such as junction chambers and drop manholes in order to construct the structure.

Flap gates and restrictor plates need to fit the structure to which they are to be attached.

Flap gates in ditch bottoms prohibit the required movement.

Jack Schmitt, P.E.

Maintenance of ditch flow during culvert replacement may require additional Pay Items, temporary pipes or detention facilities.

Connections to combined sewer systems are regulated by municipalities and may require permits and unique calculations.

The collection of ditch flow into an enclosed storm system will introduce sediment and can affect the design flow.

The control of inverts during jacking operations requires specified tolerances and may result in an unintended alteration of the hydraulics.

Sewer sizes cannot pass through all appurtenances.

Inlets in approach slabs or transitional pavements require additional details, reinforcement or construction procedures.

Storm sewers and under drains that are shown to pass through temporary retaining walls and sheet piling can result in issues.

Staking beyond construction limits for culverts or other underground facilities may require easements or extended traffic control.

Restrictor plates and flap gates that exceed the proposed structure dimensions may result in a change order.

Grading

The use of significant decimal places needs to reflect the materials that are to be graded, e. g. sand, clay dumped stone and topsoil all present different challenges to setting finished elevations.

It is necessary to avoid the placement of grade stakes set in standing water or in paved areas.

Inverts that are buried by proposed grading will not operate as intended.

Manholes that protrude from side slopes may result in an obstacle to be protected from errant vehicles or maintenance operations.

Ditch flow lines cannot collect under-drain outlets whose inverts are below the ditch grades when constructed per plan detail.

Changes in grades may not match haul calculations.

Plans, Special Provisions and Contract Plan Reviews

Unintended tree removal may be caused by grading slopes.
Back-pitching of driveways may result in trapped water.
Side slopes can block under-drain outlets or pipe culvert end sections.
Embankment placed in standing water may affect compaction.
Improper drainage of the sub-grade can present compaction issues.
Trapped water at the sides of driveways may require culverts.
Parkway and driveway slopes that contradict will affect grading.
Contours lines do not cross each other.

Utilities

Utility companies can change ownership during the course of design.
There is a difference between public and private utilities.
Compare utility atlases with survey data.
Actual field utility locates may vary from the atlas.
Vertical clearances to overhead wires need to be noted.
Define method for holding pipes or utilities that cross each other.
Seasonal requirements may affect utility relocation.
Service boxes can be exposed by ditch grading.
Some municipalities may have a priority ranking for utility work.
Service connections from a main to a customer might not be shown.
Water main cannot pass through storm manholes without permit.
The proposed size of water main or sanitary sewer is needed.
Sheet piling cannot pass through utilities.
Power pole bracing across driveways and sidewalks impedes use.

Cross-Sections

Clearing and topsoil removal will alter the existing ground.
Compare each cross section with the Typical Sections.

Jack Schmitt, P.E.

Stockpiles of borrow material, salvaged topsoil and cleared vegetation may affect cross-sections.

The economics of hauling are based on the profile and cross sections.

Placing embankment on broken pavement to remain in place may affect quantities, compaction, drainage or utilities.

Removal of unsuitable material and replacement with selected material require end section measurements.

Removal of sidewalk may be due to back slope or sewer replacement.

Fine grading near bridge abutments may expose the structure.

Compaction on top of installed underground pipes, sewers, water-mains may result in damage, deflection or breakage.

Trench backfill deductions may affect embankment quantities.

Trenching for sewers may result in unintended removal of pavement.

Ditch excavation may expose utilities.

Shrinkage factors vary by region.

Erosion control measure may alter existing ground surfaces.

Structural excavation and pavement removal need to be separate from earth excavation to ensure accurate quantities.

Lifts and benching for embankment placement need to be specified.

Embankment to be placed on slopes may require benching.

Pavement or structural removal may include sub-grade material.

Runoff repairs on embankment may require additional material.

The use of lime modification in wetland areas and on porous granular backfill results in construction issues.

Backs of curbs need to match or a transition will be needed.

Elevations at the limits of construction must match.

Trapped water conditions can easily be seen in cross sections.

Definition of ditch bottoms for rip-rap areas is required.

Plans, Special Provisions and Contract Plan Reviews

Flow of water from railroad ballasts differs from slope runoff.
Cross Sections may be required at detention ponds.
Drainage patterns on grading need to match.
Beginning /end improvement needs to match the existing conditions.
Work beyond ROW requires easement or property acquisition.
Paved areas can be compared with locations of sheet piling.

Construction Details

Identify where the stationing of a construction item is to be found.
Elements of roadside barriers have dimensions which combine for a specific length.
Height of fence and type of fence posts need to be defined.
Storm sewers need to fit beneath proposed pavement.
Pavement patching requires several operations such as sawing, grinding, dowel bar installation or hand-compaction.
Rumble strips on shoulders may be a pay item.
Details for gore areas may not fit the project limits.
Bridge approach pavement constructed in stages may need detailing.
Concrete barrier base is not placed on top of aggregate shoulder.
Depth of under drain is often below proposed ditch.
Details may require specific components, joints, safety steps, surface treatment, clearance from obstacles, etc.
Driveway construction differs between communities.

Traffic Signals

Temporary traffic signals that are erected in locations of proposed construction result in staging conflicts.
Visibility of temporary traffic signals can be impaired by proposed bridges, sign trusses, landscaping or road geometry.
Bracing for temporary poles cannot cross driveways.

Span wires and poles crossing or erected on private property may require easements or agreements.

Traffic controllers are often unintentionally placed in ditches.

Surface grinding can result in disabling vehicle detectors.

Emergency pre-emption needs to consider rail crossings.

Mast arm foundations are often unintentionally set in ditches or on top of sewers, drainage structures or lighting conduit.

Electrical service may not exist at the anticipated location.

Detector loops are typically not placed on bridge decks, across pavement joints or cracked pavement.

Interconnection conduit can unintentionally cross bridges, streams, driveways, streets or private property.

Hand holes placed in sloped embankment may create obstacles.

Light duty hand-holes in driveways may not withstand loads.

Conduit and cable layout may result in crossing shallow utilities.

Set the controller timing based on actual or projected traffic.

Provide foundation diameters sufficient for the intended number and size of conduits that need to be accommodated.

Foundations need to be centered for the appropriate setback from the face of curb.

The reinforcement caging needs to be checked to achieve the correct orientation of the mast arm in relation to the street.

Overhead clearances for combination poles need to be checked.

Visibility of signal heads is affected by tree-lined approaches.

Coordinate the orientation of traffic signals and pavement markings.

Grounding a traffic controller with exposed wire through a sidewalk.

Lighting

Unit duct cannot cross bridges.

Light poles cannot be placed through sewers.

Plans, Special Provisions and Contract Plan Reviews

Light foundations in ponds differ from those on solid ground.
Temporary lighting may be needed for temporary pavement.
Aerial wiring across ramps can be hit by traffic.
Length of temporary poles on side slopes affects luminaries.
Light poles placement cannot violate clear zones.
Tree removal can be caused by conduit trenching.
Light poles cannot be placed on top of manholes.

Erosion Control

A proposed fence might not fit between sidewalk and ROW.
Account for removal of temporary items at the end of construction.
Specify the disposal of sediment collected in traps.
Determine the extent of erosion control on intersecting streets.
Watch for seeding called for over paved areas.
Erosion control is needed for concrete truck wash-outs.
Repairs to erosion control may be needed after rainstorms.
Erosion of topsoil stockpiles may require erosion control.
Cleanup of tracked mud on approach or haul roads is needed.

Landscaping

Small sections of sod may be needed.
Trees may block signs.
Trees may uproot unit duct.
Topsoil, fertilizer, lime, and supplemental watering may be needed.
Selection of plant material is relative to the project climate.
Review the placement of landscaping in areas that receive salt runoff or that are used for snow storage.
Seeding cannot spill onto driveways and sidewalks.
Class of seeding may change depending on location.
Supplemental watering of sod may erode adjacent seeded areas.

Supplemental watering per plan may result in erosion control issues.

Tree root ball may not fit parkway dimensions.

Signing

Temporary or permanent sign post might pierce unit duct.
> Signing on intersecting streets may contradict proposed signs.
> Signs on ditch side-slopes may not be visible.
> Sign truss foundations can impact flow in ditches.
> Sign posts in clear zones could require protection.
> Signs on concrete light poles require strapping.

Pavement Marking

There are many different types of markings available, such as temporary markings, short term markings, painted markings, various reflective tape and sunken or attached reflectors.
> Colors and sizes of markings vary from state to state.
> Removal of temporary markings needs to be addressed.

Right-of-Way Plans

Property corners might get obliterated.
> Names of businesses could change.
> Buildings to be removed may contain a benchmark.
> Railroad rights-of-way may still be in force.
> Drainage outlets may cross into private property.

The list of possible items and issues to be reviewed is seemingly endless. Checklists might not cover all eventualities that can be encountered. It is hoped that some of the above-mentioned conditions can trigger a plan review that will result in the discovery of an anomaly that needs to be addressed in order to avoid change orders, extra work, construction issues or costly remedies.

About the Author

Jack Schmitt began his engineering experience in the U.S. Army, serving from 1967-1970 as an artillery surveyor, providing coordinate and elevation control at the division artillery level. The state-of-the-art technology at that time required the use of chaining, plumb bob, coordinates and azimuth, as well as the use of an ephemeris and transit. He served in Germany, state-side and in Vietnam.

Upon completion of his military service, Mr. Schmitt returned to college, enrolled in the cooperative education program and completed the requirements for a B.S.C.E. from Illinois Institute of Technology in 1973. His coop experiences utilized his survey skills for mapping the field layout on the I-5 extension for the Illinois State Toll Highway Authority and on stream cross-sections for a Housing and Urban Development floodplain mapping project. He developed his manual drafting skills during the preparation of contract plans for various clients, including the Cook County Highway Department, the City of Kankakee and the Illinois State Toll Highway Authority.

Mr. Schmitt's practical experience was founded upon the pre-computer-aided drafting skills required to plot topography from survey books using scales and lead holders, tee-squares and plastic triangles. The topography was then photographed for use as base mapping, from which plan sheets showing existing conditions could be developed. The proposed conditions were hand-drawn in red pencil and traced with ink on starched linen or plastic mylar sheets. Back-checking was performed using light tables or by holding one sheet on top of another against a windowpane. He was fortunate enough to spend summers on the survey crews, and winters doing design work. He also served on construction assignments as assistant resident and resident engineer on several federal-funded projects for which he provided design.

In the early 1970's, proposed design labor effort was relatively easy to estimate. The project length was sub-divided into the number of 50-scale drawings that would be required to illustrate the proposed improvement, and a factor of fifty to sixty man-hours per sheet was used to establish the entire budget, from survey through management to completion. It was not uncommon for a project team to complete one assignment and move on to the next assignment the following week. Often a single engineer would perform the design of roadway, drainage, traffic control and pavement markings, quantity calculations, special provisions, cost estimates and presentation of the plans to the client.

After receiving his P.E., he left the consulting industry to join the Illinois State Toll Highway Authority and served in a variety of staff positions in the Design Department. He served on the Presentation Committee for the annual Traffic and Highway Engineering Conference, where he helped assemble the program, selected topics of interest to engineers in both urban and rural Illinois. He developed and presented papers three years in a row (1992-1994) at the Annual Midwest Traffic Engineering and Parking Seminar, sponsored by Bradley University. At the end of his nine-year tenure with the Illinois State Toll Highway Authority, he held the title of Engineer of Design, and had reviewed the plans for over 350 projects, including the construction of I-355, the North-South Toll-Way, which was a 17-mile expressway with a multi-billion dollar budget.

Mr. Schmitt returned to the private sector, where computer-aided drafting and design was just beginning to take hold. For the next seventeen years, he served in various roles such as Operations Manager, Director of Engineering, Chief Civil Engineer and Senior Project Man-

Plans, Special Provisions and Contract Plan Reviews

ager with a number of firms. His primary duties always revolved around his talent for plan review, so that he was able to retain a hands-on role in numerous roadway projects at the municipal, county and state transportation levels.

In addition to an active participation in the field of roadway design, Mr. Schmitt was a member of the faculty of Midwest College of Engineering in Lombard, Illinois. The school was founded on the basis of presenting an engineering education using practicing engineers, rather than using members of academia. Mr. Schmitt developed courses on pavement design, highway geometrics and mass transit, and presented classes for three years, after which time the school was purchased by Illinois Institute of Technology.

He has also served since 1980 as an instructor for a variety of engineering topics, as a member of the Illinois Society of Professional Engineers (ISPE) Review Series, a refresher course for candidates taking the state licensing exam. The courses are presented as refreshers, but it has never ceased to amaze him to find that engineers can work for the four years prior to taking their licensing exam, and never hear the words "invert", "station" or "benchmark". He has traced this back to the late 1970's, when some colleges began to drop core courses such as surveying and highway design. He chaired a 70-firm consortium in a visit to the colleges that had dropped the courses. The plea from the firms was simple - "We will hire your grads, but they must have some basic knowledge of highway geometrics, roadway design and surveying". The response from the college administration was the same - "There are no research dollars available to fund studies in courses that do not change".

Since that time, he has commiserated with fellow engineers who have been forced to teach new hires the basics of roadway design, which in turn lead to the preparation of this text, intended to serve as a

Jack Schmitt, P.E.

basis for training new engineers in the fundamentals of plan preparation and content.

He was inducted into the ISPE Order of the Engineer in 2004. Mr. Schmitt is the author of a children's book, is a contributor of exam problems for NCEES, reviews courses presented to ISPE as a member of the Continuing Education Committee, reviews courses submitted for continuing education credit, reviews books for a technical publisher and has authored over a half-dozen on-line courses for continuing education credit on topics that are presented in this text. Mr. Schmitt is an Associate Value Specialist and a member of the Society of American Value Engineers, (S.A.V.E.) - Chicago Metropolitan Chapter.

www.ingramcontent.com/pod-product-compliance
Lightning Source LLC
Chambersburg PA
CBHW030749180526
45163CB00003B/954